MYTH

From Dante and Shakespeare to James Joyce and Margaret Atwood, writers have felt the need to draw on archaic narrative patterns. But if myths are just 'false stories', why do we keep telling them?

In this lively book, Laurence Coupe brings order to a vast and complex area of interest by giving any student new to the field a clear two-stage account of the study of myth. The first part, 'Reading Myth', starts from the works that most students will already know, such as Eliot's *The Waste Land* and Coppola's *Apocalypse Now*. On the basis of these, the reader is gradually acquainted with the key mythic themes, such as that of the dying god. In the second part, 'Mythic Reading', the focus is on the key mythic theories, such as those of Freud or Frye, as they might be applied to a variety of literary and cultural texts. However, it soon becomes clear that the reading of myth and the making of myth are complementary activities – 'reading myth' is also 'mythic reading'.

Coupe's overall thesis is that myth, far from being something to leave behind, as the 'rational' argument has it, is always in the process of being recreated. There is, he claims, an intimate connection between myth, language, narrative, history and imagination. Thus we can only begin to understand classic literature, contemporary film or popular song by first taking into account its mythic dimension.

Myth is an essential guide which draws on many exciting ideas comparatively new to literary and cultural theory.

Laurence Coupe is Senior Lecturer in English at Manchester Metropolitan University.

THE NEW CRITICAL IDIOM

SERIES EDITOR: JOHN DRAKAKIS, UNIVERSITY OF STIRLING

The New Critical Idiom is an invaluable series of introductory guides to today's critical terminology. Each book:

- provides a handy, explanatory guide to the use (and abuse) of the term
- offers an original and distinctive overview by a leading literary and cultural critic
- relates the term to the larger field of cultural representation.

With a strong emphasis on clarity, lively debate and the widest possible breadth of examples, *The New Critical Idiom* is an indispensable approach to key topics in literary studies.

- See below for new books in this series.

MYTH

Laurence Coupe

LONDON AND NEW YORK

First published 1997
by Routledge
11 New Fetter Lane, London EC4P 4EE

Simultaneously published in the USA and Canada
by Routledge
29 West 35th Street, New York, NY 10001

© 1997 Laurence Coupe

Typeset in Garamond and Scala Sans by Keystroke, Jacaranda Lodge,
Wolverhampton

Printed and bound in Great Britain by Clays Ltd., St. Ives PLC

British Library Cataloguing in Publication Data
A catalogue record for this book is available from the British Library

Library of Congress Cataloguing in Publication Data
Coupe, Laurence, 1950–
    Myth / Laurence Coupe.
        p.   cm. – (The new critical idiom)
    Includes bibliographical references and index.
    ISBN 0–415–13493–5 (hbk : alk. paper). – ISBN 0–415–13494–3
    (pbk. : alk. paper)
    1. Myth. I. Title. II. Series.
    BL304.C68 1997
    291.1¢3–dc21   97–7292
                                                                            CIP

ISBN 0–415–13403–5 (hbk)
ISBN 0–415–13494–3 (pbk)

For Margaret

Contents

SERIES EDITOR'S PREFACE

The New Critical Idiom is a series of introductory books which seeks to extend the lexicon of literary terms, in order to address the radical changes which have taken place in the study of literature during the last decades of the twentieth century. The aim is to provide clear, well-illustrated accounts of the full range of terminology currently in use, and to evolve histories of its changing usage.

The current state of the discipline of literary studies is one where there is considerable debate concerning basic questions of terminology. This involves, among other things, the boundaries which distinguish the literary from the non-literary; the position of literature within the large sphere of culture; the relationship between literatures of different cultures; and questions concerning the relation of literary to other cultural forms within the context of interdisciplinary studies.

It is clear that the field of literary criticism and theory is a dynamic and heterogeneous one. The present need is for individual volumes on terms which combine clarity of exposition with an adventurousness of perspective and a breadth of application. Each volume will contain as part of its apparatus some indication of the direction in which the definition of particular terms is likely to move, as well as expanding the disciplinary boundaries within which some of these terms have been traditionally contained. This will involve some re-situation of terms within the larger field of cultural representation, and will introduce examples from the area of film and the modern media in addition to examples from a variety of literary texts.

ACKNOWLEDGEMENTS

I am grateful to the following:

Talia Rodgers for her commitment to the project, and John Drakakis for his thoughtful editorship;

Philip Allan Publishers for permission to adapt material from my article, 'Reading for the Myth', which appeared in *The English Review* Volume 4, Issue 4 (April 1994);

Faber & Faber for permission to quote from the UK editions of T.S. Eliot's *Collected Poems* (1963) and Philip Larkin's *Collected Poems* (1988), Harcourt Brace & Co. for permission to quote from the US edition of the former, Farrar, Strauss & Giroux for permission to quote from the US edition of the latter, and Carcanet Press for permission to quote from Edgell Rickword's *Behind the Eyes: Collected Poems and Translations* (1976);

Michael Bell for giving me the opportunity to test my developing ideas on myth at his prestigious 'Modernism and Mythopoeia' conference (University of Warwick, April 1995), and Marc Manganaro for kindly letting me have a copy of his fascinating paper;

Don Cupitt for taking time to discuss his views on myth with me, and Robert Segal both for his advice and for setting a scholarly example which I have found inspiring but cannot claim to have followed;

my former head of department Colin Buckley for arranging a term's sabbatical for me to complete the book, my colleague Jeff Walsh for his encouragement over the years, Pam Watts for her enthusiastic support on the myth course at MMU, and other colleagues who covered my work in my absence;

Patrick O'Reilly and Trefor Thomas for invaluable practical advice and assistance, which was also offered freely by the staff of both the English and History departmental office and the All Saints Library at Manchester Metropolitan University.

INTRODUCTION

PARADIGM, PERFECTION, POSSIBILITY

Here is a story from ancient Egypt. Osiris, god of vegetation, being the object of universal love and admiration, provokes the envy of his brother Set. Set has him buried alive in a coffin, which is then thrown out to sea. Isis, goddess of vegetation, finds his body, washed up at the Lebanese port of Byblos and caught in a tree. She hides the corpse, but Set finds it and cuts it into pieces, scattering it over the land of Egypt. Isis recovers all the parts except one, the penis. Even so, having the gift of magic, she is able to make Osiris father a child, Horus. Thereafter, on ceremonial occasions the reigning king of Egypt represents Horus and the deceased king is referred to as Osiris. This story might serve as the paradigm, or exemplary pattern, of fertility myth.

Here is a second story, from ancient Mesopotamia, at the time when it was dominated by the city of Babylon. Tiamat is the primal mother goddess; she is the sea, the origin of all life; she may be imagined as a huge dragon. A younger god, Marduk, wages war with her, descending into the depths of the primordial waters to engage in hand-to-hand battle with her. Triumphing, he cuts her body into two and out of it he makes the universe. Thereafter, he is the supreme god, and the Babylonian king represents him in the annual new year festival, which takes place after the floods have subsided. This story might serve as the paradigm of creation myth.

Here is a third story, from ancient Israel. The Hebrews, later known as the Israelites, are being held captive as slaves in Egypt, and the pharoah refuses to let them go. Their god Yahweh visits the pharoah's land with ten plagues, culminating in the death of every firstborn son of every Egyptian household. The pharoah relents, and the Hebrews' leader Moses is instructed by Yahweh to lead the people to freedom through the Red Sea. No sooner have the Hebrews left Egypt, however, than the pharoah changes his mind, and sends his army after them. The waves of the sea part for the Hebrews, but join together again as the Egyptians pursue them. All the pharoah's army is drowned, while the Hebrews are able to go forward towards their promised land. Thereafter, the liberated slaves begin to understand that their god Yahweh is the one, universal and all-powerful God. They celebrate the feast of 'the Passover' to commemorate the two saving acts of Yahweh: making death 'pass over' their own households, and enabling his people to 'pass over' the Red Sea from bondage to freedom. This story might serve as the paradigm of what Northrop Frye calls the myth of 'deliverance' (Frye 1982: 49).

Here is a fourth story, from ancient Greece. King Acrisius does not want his daughter Danae to produce any children, having been told by an oracle that his grandson will grow up to kill him, and imprisons her so that she cannot possibly conceive. But the sky father Zeus enters her cell and impregnates her, and a male child is born. When the king discovers this, he shuts both his daughter and his grandson in a chest and has it thrown into the sea. Thanks to the intervention of Zeus, the chest lands safely on an island, and both mother and child are given a home by its ruler, Polydectes. As the boy Perseus grows up, he and Polydectes, who is a tyrant, become enemies. Unable to marry Danae while Perseus is present, Polydectes sends him on the almost impossible task of obtaining the head of a much feared female monster, the Medusa or Gorgon, whose gaze can turn humans to stone. With divine help he succeeds. While returning, he rescues the young woman Andromeda from a sea-dragon and takes her back with him. Upon arrival, he finds his mother in hiding from Polydectes, who is now her husband, and who has been treating her violently. Perseus turns him to stone by means of the severed head. His mother rejoices at his victory, and approves his marriage to Andromeda. Later, he does indeed kill Acrisius, throwing a discus at him by accident in the public games. This story might serve as the paradigm of hero myth.

Here is a fifth and final story, from early modern England. Prospero, duke of Milan, is deposed by his brother Antonio, who puts him and his baby daughter Miranda to sea in a rotten boat. Fortunately, they land safely on an island, where Prospero trains himself to become a magician. He frees an 'airy spirit', Ariel, from the tree where he has been imprisoned by Sycorax the witch, and he subordinates the witch's monstrous son, Caliban. Having acquired the magic arts, Prospero stages a shipwreck off the coast of the island, thus bringing his brother and his travelling companions into his power. Among these are Alonso, king of Naples, who helped Antonio in the act of deposition, and Alonso's son Ferdinand. The young man falls in love with Miranda, but before he can marry her he has to prove his worth by undergoing a kind of rite of initiation, which involves performing the hardest of menial tasks. Meanwhile his father Alonso narrowly escapes murder by his own brother Sebastian, urged on by the wicked Antonio. Moreover, he and they see a banquet appear and then disappear, thanks to Ariel, who denounces them as 'three men of sin'. Finally Alonso, who has been chastened by his experiences on the island, asks and receives forgiveness from Prospero, who extends it also to his own unrepentant brother. The king's son marries the rightful duke's daughter, and the goddesses Iris, Ceres and Juno descend to perform in the wedding masque. This story might serve as the paradigm of literary myth – or, if one prefers, mythic literature.

We have included this last example, Shakespeare's play *The Tempest* (1611), to demonstrate that the mythic and the literary are not so far apart as is often supposed. Indeed, in the chapters that follow, we will discover that 'mythology', the body of inherited myths in any culture, is an important element of literature, and that literature is a means of extending mythology. That is, literary works may be regarded as 'mythopoeic', tending to create or re-create certain narratives which human beings take to be crucial to their understanding of their world. Thus cultural and literary criticism may involve 'mythography', or the interpretation of myth, given that the mythic is an important dimension of cultural and literary experience.

But for now, it is enough to recognise that the stories told above are both similar and dissimilar. The obviously common factor is the symbolism of the sea, in each case associated paradoxically with both death and new life – as with the Christian ritual of adult baptism, in which participants feel they are dying to their former existence and being reborn from out of the water. Such a symbol is recurrent enough to be called an 'archetype' (literally, an original image, or founding figure). Equally important, though, is the narrative variation. In the first and second stories, the protagonists are divine, and their re-emergence from the waters is a sign of power. In the third and fourth stories, the protagonists are human, though either inspired or fathered by a deity, and their re-emergence from the waters is a sign of divine approval. In the fifth narrative, the protagonists are again human, but rather more so than in the third and fourth narratives: hence we might want to concentrate much more on individual characters and their interaction. However, it should be stressed that this kind of narrative presupposes the other kinds, and we are constantly aware of an overarching framework of fertility, cosmology, deliverance and superhuman heroism. The play draws its power from the existence of such paradigms, and simultaneously from its imaginative reworking of their themes. Moreover, where hero myth differs from fertility, creation and deliverance in not normally being associated with any rites, if literary myth takes the form of drama, it cannot escape the suggestion of ritual. Indeed, as with *The Tempest*, it may draw our attention to the importance of ceremony, such as Ferdinand and Miranda's wedding masque. It may well incorporate primitive ritual patterns into its own structure, such as Ferdinand's rite of initiation and Alonso's process of expiation.

Just as one particular story may serve as the paradigm for one kind of myth, so one kind of myth may serve as the paradigm for mythology itself. Mythographers, as we shall see, are fond of privileging one model over another: for Sir James Frazer, fertility myth is the key to all mythologies; for Mircea Eliade, it is creation myth. Here we will try and avoid favouring any one paradigm, adopting the 'family-resemblance' approach outlined by the theologian Don Cupitt. He considers that there are so many conflicting definitions of myth that it is least misleading to list a number of 'typical features' and then act on the assumption that a narrative is mythic if it has most, but not necessarily all, of these features. Myth is paradigmatic, but there is no pure paradigm:

> So we may say that a myth is typically a traditional sacred story of anonymous authorship and archetypal or universal significance which is recounted in a certain community and is often linked with a ritual; that it tells of the deeds of superhuman beings such as gods, demigods, heroes, spirits or ghosts; that it is set outside historical time in primal or eschatological [i.e. last, ultimate] time or in the supernatural world, or may deal with comings and goings between the supernatural world and the world of human history; that the superhuman beings are imagined in anthropomorphic [i.e. humanly formed] ways,

> although their powers are more than human and often the story
> is not naturalistic but has the fractured, disorderly logic of
> dreams; that the whole body of a people's mythology is often
> prolix [i.e. lengthy, wordy], extravagant and full of seeming
> inconsistencies; and finally that the work of myth is to explain,
> to reconcile, to guide action or to legitimate. We can add
> that myth-making is evidently a primal and universal function
> of the human mind as it seeks a more-or-less unified vision of
> the cosmic order, the social order, and the meaning of the
> individual's life. Both for society at large and for the individual,
> this story-generating function seems irreplaceable. The individual
> finds meaning in his life by making of his life a story set within
> a larger social and cosmic story.
>
> (Cupitt 1982: 29)

This 'family-resemblance' approach avoids the inevitable dogmatism of any mythography which emphasises only one paradigm. It is advisable for the mythographer to acknowledge that her own chosen emphasis is only one of many. For example, not all myths are linked with a ritual; not all myths are about gods; and not all myths concern a time outside of historical time. Exceptions to, and contradictions of, any particular paradigm are endless.

However, according to the literary critic Kenneth Burke, there is something about human language that encourages the absolutism which Cupitt advises us to avoid. Both making myths and reading myths imply a drive towards completion, an insistence on seeing things through to as near their full development as is practicable. Burke relates this tendency to the Greek philosopher Aristotle's 'entelechy' or 'actualisation of potential', the process by which an acorn insists, as it were, on becoming a full-grown oak, or a child insists on becoming a mature adult. Burke's equivalent term is 'perfectionism', but he is much more sceptical about the principle than the casual reader might think. Above all, he insists that in considering myth we trace the stages by which the idea of perfection is generated and sustained. This will inevitably involve some hypothesis, since few people can claim to have been present when a myth was invented.

Thus the first stage might be 'some material operation to be performed, such as the planting, cultivating and harvesting of crops', involving a 'strictly pragmatic use of speech', a simple 'saying' to accompany the 'doing' (such as 'Pass me those seeds'). The second stage might be the completed harvest. The third stage might be the desire to 'double' or 'round out' the experience through story and symbolism, to charge it with significance, which finds expression in myth and ritual. If the context is that of planting and reaping, then we will get fertility myth and ritual, involving a god of vegetation and a sacrifice. The fourth stage might be the designation by the community of certain 'myth men' or 'mythic specialists' (priests or magicians) who conserve and communicate the myth and who supervise the ritual in their apparently pure form. Fifthly, the readers of the myth, distant in time and space from its creators, might take the myth to be the complete answer to their theoretical problems. Thus for both originators and interpreters, myth might offer, for the duration of the narrative, not just a provisional paradigm but an approximation to totality (Burke 1971: 100–5).

Burke does not argue against this hypothetical process, but reminds us that it is usually a good idea when dealing with a myth to consider what it is 'doing' as well as what it is 'saying': that is, to bear in mind the pragmatic impulse which would have occasioned it in the first place. The same applies when we are dealing with an interpretation of myth: if the interpreter has decided in advance one dominant meaning of myth, then she has projected a certain idea of perfection onto material that may have more practical functions. But then, all this is to be expected, and to be understood rather than condemned outright, for the human being is 'the symbol-using animal' who, as such, is 'goaded by the spirit of hierarchy': that is, 'moved by a sense of order', or having 'the incentives of organisation and status'. Put more strongly, this same animal is 'rotten with perfection', which is both a blessing and a curse. It is a blessing because it allows us to conceive of the 'perfect' season, and so the 'perfect' harvest, and so, if that is what we want, the 'perfection' of myth. It is a curse because it also allows us to conceive of the 'perfect' victim or scapegoat, and so the 'perfection' of sacrifice. Pushed further, it may result in such phenomena of our century as the 'perfect' enemy to be exterminated by the master race (as in the rhetoric of Adolf Hitler) or the construction of the 'perfect' thermo-nuclear warhead (Burke 1966: 15–22). Thus the drive towards completion and unity can create not only powerfully imaginative stories but also systematic violence. Myth may imply totality, but 'perfectionism' is to be resisted where it becomes totalitarian.

Thus far we have defined myth in relation to the notion of the paradigm, and again to that of perfection. But there is a third aspect to be considered, perhaps less sceptically than the first two – that of possibility. Here we take our cue from the philosopher Paul Ricoeur, who argues that we must go beyond the modern view of myth as 'false explanation' to a sense of its 'exploratory significance and its contribution to understanding'. He speaks of the 'symbolic function' of myth, its power of discovery and revelation. Though he agrees with Burke that the impetus of myth can be explained, he does not agree with the more usual assumption of the modern age, that myth as such can be explained away. For its purpose may always exceed its origin; as a stimulus to speculation, it is a genuine 'dimension of modern thought' (Ricoeur 1967: 5). Moreover, myth may imply a hierarchy, but it also implies a horizon: it is 'a disclosure of unprecedented worlds, an opening on to other *possible* worlds which transcend the established limits of our *actual* world' (Ricoeur 1991: 490). In other words, while myth may be paradigmatic, and while it may imply a social and cosmic order, or perfection, it also carries with it a promise of another mode of existence entirely, to be realised just beyond the present time and place. It is not only foundational (as in fertility and creation narratives) but also liberating (as in deliverance and in many heroic and literary narratives).

THE MYTH OF MYTHLESSNESS

Paradigm, perfection and possibility: these, then, are three terms to bear in mind when approaching myth. But the third raises in turn another issue, for Ricoeur is only having to defend myth because it is being attacked. In short, he is countering that movement known as 'demythologisation'. We usually associate this with modernity, but as Jean-Pierre Vernant explains, it goes back a good deal further:

> The concept of myth that we have inherited from the Greeks belongs, by reason of its origins and history, to a tradition of thought peculiar to Western civilisation in which myth is defined in terms of what is not myth, being opposed to reality (myth is fiction) and, secondly, to what is rational (myth is absurd). If the development of the study of myth in modern times is to be understood it must be considered in the context of this line of thought and tradition.
>
> (Vernant 1982: 186)

It was the second opposition, that of myth and rationality, which proved the more decisive. 'Myth' originally meant 'speech' or 'word', but in time what the Greeks called *mythos* was separated out from, and deemed inferior to, *logos*. The former came to signify fantasy; the latter, rational argument. This process was a tortuous one, but the result was crucial:

> Between the eighth and fourth centuries B.C. a whole series of interrelated conditions caused a multiplicity of differentiations, breaks and internal tensions within the mental universe of the Greeks which were responsible for distinguishing the domain

> of myth from other domains: the concept of myth peculiar to classical antiquity thus became clearly defined through the setting up of an opposition between *muthos* [sic] and *logos*, henceforth seen as separate and contrasting terms.
>
> (Vernant 1982: 187)

However, we are not to infer that late antiquity witnessed a wholesale demythologization. As Thomas Altizer indicates, the need for myth was clearly evident in the 'higher' religions, as we can tell from the numerous narratives of creation, fertility and deliverance. Moreover, if there was an attempt by classical Greek philosophy to distinguish itself from myth, it was ambivalent: Plato is justly famous for his fables.

As we shall see, it was during the Enlightenment, that glorification of reason which dominated the later seventeenth and early eighteenth centuries, that a systematic attempt was made to explain away mythology. But demythologization has also enjoyed a revival in the twentieth century. The German theologian Rudolf Bultmann (1884–1976) wanted to rescue the Christian Bible, which was for him the scripture of the very highest religion, from the misconceptions and fantasies of a 'pre-scientific' outlook. What he advised was, first recognising the debt which St Paul and the Gospel-writers owed to mythology, then separating out the saving message or *kerygma* of Jesus Christ hidden beneath or behind it. In his long essay 'New Testament and Mythology' he explains that the mythic cosmos informing the Epistles and the Gospels is a 'three-storied structure', consisting of a heaven above, a hell below and an earth in the middle. 'The earth is the scene of the supernatural activity of God and his angels on the one hand, and of Satan and his demons on the other. These supernatural forces intervene in the course of nature and in all that men think and will and do' (Bultmann 1953: 1). Like Burke, Bultmann emphasises the hierarchical aspect of mythic thinking; but unlike Burke he thinks it can be disposed of. Modern humanity does not need to think in terms of a cosmic battle between God and Satan. Of course, to be fair to Bultmann, he is not simply repudiating *mythos* in the name of *logos*: rather, he is updating it in order that the *Logos*, the Word of God, is not obscured. That is, he is seeking to translate the mythological content of the Gospels into modern, existential meaning. The *kerygma*, the hidden message concerning the *Logos*, is what matters, and the narrative medium must be rendered in non-narrative, immediate terms for it to speak anew to the individual Christian of today. Thus his business might be better described, not as demythologization but as de-literalisation. However, either way the effect is the same, and what we end up with is an imaginatively impoverished text, consisting of only what speaks directly to the twentieth-century reader's 'experience' (Bultmann's term).

Only a year or two after a theologian had been arguing for an attitude of suspicion towards ancient myth, a poet was expressing his distaste for that literary legacy which he called the 'myth-kitty'. Interestingly, he too spoke of the need to get close to 'experience' and not to obscure one's vision with legendary references and fanciful associations. Like Bultmann, Philip Larkin was speaking the language of modernity. If we substitute 'experience' for *logos*, we can see from his 'Statement' (1955) that he too belongs to the history of demythologization. From this we are to infer that allusions to sacred tales are what another and inferior kind of poet, probably pretentious and certainly confused, goes for. Larkin will remain true to the real world: 'I write poems to preserve things I have seen/thought/felt (if I may so indicate a composite and complex experience) both for myself and for others, which I am trying to keep from oblivion for its own sake.' Larkin thus has 'no belief' in 'a common myth-kitty', which only serves as a distraction from the task of communication (Larkin 1983: 79). Like Bultmann, Larkin here is seeking the authenticity of pure individual experience, which he opposes to a cultural legacy equated with mere convention and even obfuscation.

But there is a limit to the lyrical empiricism of Larkin. Very few of his poems actually confine themselves to the truth of the everyday. We may note how often they culminate in a mood of extreme yearning for some saving paradigm. 'The Whitsun Weddings' begins as a matter-of-fact observation of young couples boarding the train for their honeymoons, but ends by invoking the spirit of fertility, from which the speaker feels painfully alienated – the sexual image of 'an arrow-shower' merging with the prospect of 'rain' (Larkin 1988: 116). The short lyric 'The Trees' makes the same appeal to the fertility paradigm, only more explicitly. The speaker, conscious of growing older, wants to believe that the trees signify regeneration, that they are urging us to 'Begin afresh, afresh, afresh' (Larkin 1988: 166). Here the fertility overlaps with the creation paradigm, by which a new world is felt to begin. In 'High Windows' the latter dominates. Disgusted by the shallow pleasures of this world, the speaker seems to ask to be lifted up into a higher realm. The cosmology here is spatial, indeed hierarchical: the 'thought of high windows' implies, beyond the 'sun-comprehending glass' a 'deep blue air' which, being 'nowhere' on this earth, is 'endless' (Larkin 1988: 165). Accepting Proust's observation that the only paradise is indeed the one that has been lost, it would not perhaps be inappropriate to regard Larkin's poetry as mythic in the sense of seeking to evoke an absent plenitude of being. It is about the lack of the sacred, the desire for totality. It is haunted by what Larkin himself names 'The Importance of Elsewhere'. It reeks of myth as surely as the kind of allusive writing, so circumspect about tradition, that he explicitly repudiates in the name of 'experience'. There is indeed experience in Larkin, but it is the experience of absence. Where he appears to be expressing himself directly in the first person on a personal matter, he is really reproducing an inherited narrative of longing. Myth and mythopoeia have survived the individual attempt at demythologisation.

If we need a phrase to sum up the error of modernity, represented here by Bultmann and (as critic) by Larkin, we might do worse than use that of Robert Jewett and John Shelton Lawrence: 'the myth of mythlessness'. By this they mean the unexamined belief which arose in the Enlightenment and which still survives: the belief that humanity has successfully transcended the need for mythical forms of thought (Jewett and Lawrence 1977: 250). This arrogant view, already thrown into doubt by Cupitt, Burke and Ricoeur, will be further challenged in the chapters that follow.

I

READING MYTH

INTRODUCTION
TO PART I

It is always possible to read a literary or cultural text for its mythic interest. This inevitably presupposes that other texts are of related interest, since one is chiefly involved in tracing commonly accepted paradigms. Comparison and contrast thus come into play. But of course these activities in turn depend on how one reads myth in the first place: that is, on which paradigms are of interest, and on how to interpret them. What is called 'myth criticism' is inseparable from what is called 'mythography'. The latter has usually been a matter of giving priority to one particular paradigm; here we will be drawing attention to the implications of doing so.

In this part we will be offering an exercise in myth criticism which begins and ends with Francis Ford Coppola's film about the Vietnam war, *Apocalypse Now* (1979). By the logic just outlined, we will find that, rather than inviting a lengthy and detailed analysis, this work will soon lead us to others. For we cannot understand *Apocalypse Now* as a mythic text unless we refer it back to *The Golden Bough*; and it is almost impossible to deal with

Frazer's major work of mythography in this context without referring to the poem on which it had the most famous influence, Eliot's *The Waste Land* (1922). Nor can the latter be situated without taking note of Eliot's own case for 'the mythical method'; which in turn makes more sense when we juxtapose it with the mythopoeic programme of his contemporary, Edgell Rickword. The latter's interest in the Symbolist poet and visionary, Arthur Rimbaud, connects him with Jim Morrison, lyricist of the Doors. Moroever, the presence of their music on the soundtrack of *Apocalypse Now* invites us to ponder the relation between contemporary popular culture and mythopoeia. And by connotation our enquiry will extend to encompass also Michael Herr's *Dispatches*, which explores the Vietnam war as a myth, and the theories of Mircea Eliade, which help situate both Eliot and Morrison. Eventually, we will return to where we started, with *Apocalypse Now*, this time concentrating on the significance of its title. This will necessitate a brief account of the Book of Revelation and its influence. That will take us to the end of Part I, and in Part II we will reconsider some of the theoretical issues raised in a wider historical perspective. We will move from 'reading myth' to 'mythic reading': that is, we will make explicit the intimate connection between 'mythography', the interpretation of myth, and 'mythopoeia', the making of myths.

Broadly, Chapter 1 will focus on the paradigm of fertility myth, as expounded by Frazer, and on the way it is put at the service of a particular view of hierarchy in the poetry and criticism of Eliot. In Chapter 2 we will consider the resonance of the paradigm of creation myth, as expounded by Eliade; but we will approach this topic dialectically, by addressing the 'chaos' which is presupposed by 'cosmos'. This dimension will be mainly represented by the poems and songs of Jim Morrison of The Doors. In Chapter 3, the paradigm will be that of the myth of deliverance, as variously expressed and explored in ancient and modern narrative, and in creative and critical work. Throughout, hero myths will be addressed where appropriate. Always the emphasis will be on the relation of all these to literary and cultural texts.

In what follows, it will be as well to bear in mind some distinctions which are normally observed in literary and cultural history: in particular, modernity, modernism, postmodernity and postmodernism. We have already said that demythologization is associated with 'modernity'. The name for the aesthetic movement which resisted this trend is 'modernism'. Though the two terms are often used interchangeably, it makes much more sense to see them rather as dialectical opposites. Wherever myth has been pronounced dead, artists have risen up to proclaim it alive. One such was T.S. Eliot. But of course *The Waste Land* was a long time ago, and with the emergence of 'postmodernity', or 'the postmodern condition', we have witnessed, not a retreat from myth, but a much more pervasive sense of myth. Where Eliot sought to counter history by invoking antique form, for the 'postmodernist' artist such as Francis Ford Coppola the response demanded by contemporary culture is to blur the distinction between history and myth, as in *Apocalypse Now*.

1

ORDER

DYING GODS

Coppola's *Apocalypse Now* was inspired initially by Joseph Conrad's *Heart of Darkness* (1902), which indeed informs the film throughout. The narrator, in the former named Willard and in the latter Marlow, takes a terrifying river journey. In the novella this is along the Congo in the days of the imperialist scramble for Africa; in the film it is through Vietnam to Cambodia during the American war against the Vietcong. He is trying to locate a mysterious figure, in both cases called Kurtz, whose mind has apparently been deranged by his years in the wilderness. Kurtz has become the object of native worship, and has encouraged the most barbaric practices. The film goes beyond Conrad's tale in that Captain Willard of the US Army has received instructions to 'terminate with extreme prejudice' the command of Colonel Kurtz – that is, kill him – because his 'methods' are 'unsound'. In other words, his mission is the murder of a man who has set himself up as a god. This murder is performed in parallel with the natives' sacrifice of a buffalo. In both novella and film, Kurtz's last words are: 'The horror! the horror!' But where Marlow returns to England to persuade the fiancée of this 'universal genius' that his final utterance was her name, Willard leaves Kurtz's temple to be faced by his followers' bowing down before him, as the new god. Refusing this role, he leaves the settlement; the final sequence, seen over the closing credits, shows it being bombed by American helicopters.

Coppola, then, gives to Conrad's narrative the power of a mythic paradigm. Here the choice is that of fertility myth, and his guides are Sir James Frazer and Jessie L. Weston. Thus it is no coincidence that his Kurtz, the man-god condemned to die, has in his possession those two works by them which deal with that very topic. Conveniently, when the camera pans the interior of Kurtz's temple, it lingers on these volumes, ensuring the viewer registers their relevance. They are Frazer's *The Golden Bough* and Weston's *From Ritual to Romance*. If Conrad's novella provides Coppola with his storyline, it is these exercises in mythography which provide him with his structure. We will call this the pattern of the dying and reviving god.

The Golden Bough appeared in twelve volumes between 1890 and 1915, and was subsequently abridged in one volume in 1922. Its subtitle is 'A study in magic and religion'. This monumental work is organised like a detective novel, since it begins with a murder and then sets out to identify the murderer and, more importantly for Frazer, the motive and the method. Sabine McCormack, who has edited a new abridgement of Frazer's lengthy and tortuous account, sets the scene:

> At Nemi, near Rome, there was a shrine where, down to imperial times, Diana, goddess of woodlands and animals and giver of offspring, was worshipped with a male consort, Virbius. The rule of the shrine was that any man could be its priest, and take the title of the King of the Wood, provided he first plucked a branch – the Golden Bough – from a certain sacred tree in

the temple grove and then killed the priest. This was the regular mode of succession to the priesthood. The aim of *The Golden Bough* is to answer two questions: why did the priest have to kill his predecessor, and why did he first have to pluck the branch?

Because there is no simple answer to either question, Frazer collects and compares analogies to the custom of Nemi. For by showing that similar rules existed all over the world and throughout history, he hopes to reach an understanding of how the primitive mind works, and then to use his understanding to shed light on the rule of Nemi. In collecting analogies, Frazer does not look for total parallels, but breaks up the custom of Nemi into its component parts and examines each in turn. Indeed, one piece of evidence may be used for more than one aspect of the question.

(Frazer 1978: 18)

Thus Frazer's anthropology may be categorised, firstly, as belonging to the 'myth and ritual' school of interpretation. As the epithet suggests, this approach to mythology explains the narrative in terms of the ceremony which, it is assumed, it arose from or accompanied. As the kind of ceremony Frazer is most interested in is that of vegetation, the kind of myth he is most interested in is that concerning a fertility god and goddess. Having chosen that model, he chooses as the paradigm of his paradigm the Phoenician/Greek story of Adonis – which he takes to be analogous to the story of Osiris, which we have already encountered. The myth tells us that, as a man, Adonis is mortally wounded by a wild boar, to be subsequently revived as a god by Aphrodite, the goddess of love and fertility (the Roman Venus). The idea is that she wishes to ensure that each year he will be reborn in the spring to be with her. Frazer describes the ritual interest of this story:

At the festivals of Adonis, which were held in Western Asia and in Greek lands, the death of the god was annually mourned, with a bitter wailing, chiefly by women; images of him, dressed to resemble corpses, were carried out as to burial and then thrown into the sea or into springs; and in some places his revival was celebrated on the following day. At Alexandria images of Aphrodite and Adonis were displayed on two couches; beside them were set ripe fruits of all kinds, cakes, plants growing in flower-pots, and green bowers twined with anise. The marriage of the lovers was celebrated one day, and on the morrow women attired as mourners, with streaming hair and bared breasts, bore the image of the dead Adonis to the sea-shore and committed it to the waves. Yet they sorrowed not without hope, for they sang that the lost one would come back again.

(Frazer 1978: 130)

The meaning of such a ritual, and such a myth, is fertility. This, as we shall see, is what links it with the rule of Nemi.

Which brings us to the second aspect of Frazer's anthropology: it employs the 'comparative method'. All places and times, any odd scraps of evidence of ritual practice, are grist to the mill. Material may be gleaned from nineteenth-century England as legitimately as ancient Greece. Anywhere there is a residue of fertility ritual (for example, an effigy thrown into a river then fished out again), the overall pattern of death and regeneration may be inferred. Frazer is, that is to say, a 'universalist': he believes that we can make comparisons across cultures because the primitive human urge to myth-making is essentially the same. Of course, his very claim to be able to do so suggests something of the spirit of modernity. The ceremonies and stories documented belong either to our archaic past or to the residual barbarism of the 'folk' imagination. Thus, though Frazer's ostensible interest is mythographic not mythopoeic, his very condescension towards the evidence he universalises betrays the myth at work: derived from the Enlightenment, it is the story of progress via rationality. We have already named this as the 'myth of mythlessness'. That is one paradox at the heart of Frazer's work. Another is that, despite subscribing to his own narrative of improvement, he betrays a nostalgia for the world which produced the ceremonies and stories he recovers in such painstaking detail. That is, while Frazer's official position is something very close to positivism, envisaging humanity as having progressed from magic, through religion, and so to science, he seems almost as fascinated by what he calls the 'folly' of the first two stages as by the supposed truth of the third.

But let us be sure how 'myth and ritual' interpretation and universalist comparativism work in practice. In short, we must register Frazer's answers to Frazer's own questions. Why does the King of the Wood have to die? Why does the successor have to pluck the branch? After twelve volumes, we have the answers. The god, or his impersonator, has to die precisely because his business is fertility. The community depends on him, or so it believes, for its own survival. If the god does not die he cannot be reborn to fertilise the goddess, and so there will be no new crops. The underlying principle is that of magic, which for Frazer is the origin of all myth-making and all religion. Indeed, he goes further, and credits magic with the beginnings of secular authority, and so of civilisation itself; not only the first priests but the first kings were evidently magicians. The succession to the title of King of the Wood was a matter of magic, elaborated as religious ritual.

According to Frazer, at the early, magical stage of thinking, nature is conceived as an impersonal force, to be manipulated. As magic becomes religion, nature takes on the form of anthropomorphic deities, who must be allowed full scope to exercise their powers. Everything comes to hinge on guaranteeing the god his fertility. The residual logic is twofold. By 'sympathetic' magic, the death and revival of the god parallels or, to put it more strongly, causes the renewal of the land. (Frazer compares this with the act of pouring water on the ground in order to induce rain.) By 'contagious' magic, the god becomes a 'scapegoat' figure who carries away the sterility which might otherwise blight the crops. (Strictly speaking, this is 'anti-contagious' magic. Frazer illustrates contagious magic itself by the lover winning power over the beloved by casting a spell on clippings of her hair.) The logic is foolproof. And it tells us also why the King of the Wood must pluck 'the Golden Bough'. This part of the tree, which is an oak, is clearly the mistletoe. It contains the power of Jupiter, Roman god of sky and storm, who periodically casts his full force into the tree in the course of a lightning flash. The successor to the title must pluck it in order to prove he has acquired the divine energy. Only through this violent succession, anticipated by the violence of the thunderstorm, can the fertility of the land be ensured. There is a magical connection between the drama of the dying and reviving god on the one hand, and the seasonal cycle on the other. The king is dead; long live the king.

If the basis of religion is the pattern of death and regeneration, then it is possible to conclude that the 'higher' faiths cannot claim exemption from this paradigm. Indeed, in the first edition of *The Golden Bough* it is quite obvious that Frazer began by regarding Jesus Christ as just another variant upon the model of the dying and reviving god. As the work progressed, however, he became increasingly evasive on this issue – as though Frazer, a mild agnostic, were fearful of excessive controversy. But the connection between fertility religion and Christianity did need spelling out, and his disciple Jessie L. Weston broached the issue directly. Or rather, she sought to demonstrate that narratives which had previously been taken to be purely Christian had in fact originated in vegetation ceremonies, or what she called 'Nature Cults'. Reading Weston's *From Ritual to Romance* (1920), we see how Frazer's anthropology can help solve long-standing puzzles of literary interpretation – in this case, that the medieval legend of the Holy Grail is not anticipated by Christian orthodoxy:

> Some years ago, when fresh from the study of Sir J.G. Frazer's epoch-making work, *The Golden Bough*, I was struck by the resemblance existing between certain features of the Grail story, and characteristic details of the Nature Cults described. The more closely I analysed the tale, the more striking became the resemblance, and I finally asked myself whether it were not possible that in this mysterious legend – mysterious alike in its character, its sudden appearance, the importance apparently assigned to it, followed by as sudden and complete a disappearance – we might not have the confused record of a ritual, once popular, later surviving under conditions of strict secrecy?
>
> (Weston 1920: 3–4)

Weston's assumption is that the fertility ritual documented by Frazer was transformed in time into a 'Mystery Cult'. Certainly, it is true that in the centuries immediately before and after Christ, the ancient near east and the Mediterranean region witnessed a religious displacement. The collective festival ensuring the revival of the crops, and so the survival of the community, was intermittently adapted into a new kind of ceremony. In this kind, the individual initiate sought liberation from the chains of earthly life, putting trust not in a fertility god such as Adonis or Osiris, but in a 'mystery' god such as Attis.

The story of Attis is that he is a Phrygian shepherd driven mad by the goddess Cybele's love for him; in his frenzy he castrates himself, only to be taken up by her as her eternal consort (often depicted riding with her on a chariot drawn by lions). The cult, which spread throughout Greece and then to Rome, centred on an annual, spring ritual in honour of Attis: this would involve devotees' castrating themselves, and there would also be group

flagellation by priests dressed as women. After this, the participants would celebrate the rebirth of the god. Recounted like this,
the ritual seems similar to that of Adonis, but Weston's argument
is that there was a much stronger emphasis on initiation.
Those dedicated to Attis were distinguished from the populace
generally by their willingness to emasculate themselves. In other
words, there were two levels of worship: 'exoteric' (by which the
community at large benefited from Attis' rebirth) and 'esoteric'
(by which the chosen few participated in the secret of his
divinity). In this respect, the worship of Attis brought it very close
to 'the Eleusian mysteries' – Eleusis being the site of a temple in
honour of Demeter, goddess of corn, and the mysteries involving
a two-stage initiation. The first involved symbolism of vegetation;
the second took a less tangible form, but supposedly led to a
profounder, more spiritual insight.

For some time, evidently, Jesus Christ was identified as a mystery
god, effecting salvation on two levels. For the many he would be
just another dying god of vegetation; for the few he would be the
object of secret devotion. The link between the two levels would be
the 'Messianic' or 'Eucharistic' feast, in which the bread and wine
could be regarded not only as the harvest and the vintage but also
as spiritual nourishment. Hence the symbolism of the Grail:

> It has taken me nine or ten years longer to complete the
> evidence, but the chain is at last linked up, and we can now
> prove by printed texts the parallels existing between each and
> every feature of the Grail story and the recorded symbolism of
> the Mystery Cults. Further, we can show that between these
> Mystery Cults and Christianity there existed at one time a
> close and intimate union, such a union as of itself involved
> the practical assimilation of the central rite, in each case a
> 'Eucharistic' Feast, in which the worshippers partook of the
> Food of Life from the sacred vessels.

> (Weston 1920: 4–5)

Weston's conclusion, made with due acknowledgement to Frazer, is that the Grail legend derived from the 'Mystery Cult' just as surely as the 'Mystery Cult' derived from the 'Nature Cult'. The later literary form of romance, which in the case of the Grail narratives involved the quest of a knight for the lost cup containing Christ's sacrificial blood, was firmly rooted in fertility religion; only it had developed by way of a detour through mystery. What was constant was the idea of the body and blood of the saviour offering new life, whether the communal life of fertility or the individual life of enlightenment.

The parallel with Frazer's material is striking. We know from Frazer that there is no question that the existing King of the Wood has to be replaced by a violent usurper – probably a desperate, runaway slave – full of new potency for the fertilisation of the goddess. Otherwise life will not come out of death, spring out of winter. Similarly, Weston argues, the questing knight is given a definite series of tasks in a definite order. He has to undergo terrible ordeals, such as that of the 'Chapel Perilous'. He has to find the Grail castle. He has to ask the ritual question of the chalice: 'Whom does it serve?' He has to understand the answer: that the wounded 'Fisher King' and the 'Waste Land' are one. Only by his doing so will the healing powers of the Grail be effective: the waters freed, the monarch healed and fertility restored. Finally, with the Waste Land redeemed, its ruler is able to die in peace, and the quester can become the new Fisher King. Nor is it a matter simply of ensuring the regeneration of the land. What has ailed the king has, it seems, been a crisis of spirit, a lack of faith in the efficacy of the Grail. The successful knight, usually named Perceval or Parsifal, represents the power of innocent wisdom. He replaces Anfortas, the wounded or impotent monarch, suffering from the infirmity of misunderstanding. Thus we have glimpsed a mysterious initiation, founded in vegetation ceremony and embellished by not only the folk imagination but also centuries of spiritual speculation. We have moved thereby from sacred ceremony ('Ritual') to secular literature ('Romance').

Coppola's Kurtz may be understood in the light of both *The Golden Bough* and *From Ritual to Romance*. He may be identified with the ageing King of the Wood, killed by the younger man, namely Willard. However, here the usurpation does not lead to renewal; death does not lead to new life. Willard refuses the role of king, and departing from Kurtz's community, effectively gives the all-clear for its destruction. The 'myth and ritual' structure has been used, but with severe irony. Moreover, in this mythic text, the pattern does not include the goddess. If she is present at all, it is in the triple form of three *Playboy* models whose entertainment for the troops consists in exciting them to futile sexual frenzy. The Vietnam war is the antithesis of fertility. As for Weston's questing knight and Fisher King: Willard and Kurtz may play these parts, the former undergoing all manner of ordeals during his quest for Kurtz's temple and the latter displaying all the signs of spiritual sickness; but again, no succession takes place, and from Willard's traumatised expression at the end of the film, no enlightenment has been gained. Again, the mythic material is used ironically. Yet the irony, judging by the cult status of Coppola's film, only intensifies the mythic appeal. One meets few devotees of the film who are also advocates of demythologization.

WORDS AND THE WORD

> I decided that the ending could be the classic myth of the murderer who goes up the river, kills the king and then himself becomes the king – it's the Fisher King, from The Golden Bough. Somehow it's the granddaddy of all myths . . . . [In] reading some of The Golden Bough and then From Ritual to Romance I found a lot concerning that theme. T.S. Eliot's The Wasteland also seemed so apt for the conclusion of the story.
>
> (Cowie 1990: 123)

Whatever the confusions in Coppola's acknowledgement of influence – for instance, locating the story of the Fisher King in *The Golden Bough* – this quotation is a useful indicator of the link he had understood between Frazer, Weston and Eliot before finding an appropriately mythic conclusion for *Apocalypse Now*. Here we will not be trying to demonstrate the influence of Eliot on Coppola, which is evident enough from Kurtz's recitation from 'The Hollow Men' in the darkness of his temple, but simply making sure that *The Waste Land* is understood in its own right, as the poem at the heart of modernist mythopoeia. Then, when we come to consider Coppola's film again, at the end of Part I, we will be in a position to appreciate how Eliot's project differs, despite its undoubted influence, from the more diffuse sense of myth that characterises postmodernism.

Eliot, taking his cue perhaps from Conrad, argued that literature had to face the 'horror' of modern life. And, since 'horror' could only be appreciated intermittently, it had to alternate with 'boredom'. But beyond both, there was a need for what he called 'glory' (Eliot 1964: 106). The work which best illustrates this thinking is *The Waste Land* itself. Its irony, its fascination with 'boredom' and 'horror', only articulates the loss of, and need for, 'glory'. It is a poem which, despite its reputation for obscurity and experimentation, is thoroughly informed by what Burke calls 'perfectionism': it centres on the need for hierarchy, completion, order. The means to this for Eliot is the paradigm of fertility. As he himself confirms in the notes accompanying the poem, it is informed by the 'myth and ritual' school of interpretation. He explictly acknowledges his debt to *The Golden Bough* and *From Ritual to Romance*, the latter in particular suggesting not only 'the title' but also 'the plan and a good deal of the incidental symbolism'. He adds that anyone acquainted with Frazer's and Weston's books 'will immediately recognise in the poem certain references to vegetation ceremonies' (Eliot 1963: 80).

Perhaps we should emphasise here the deliberateness of the

poet's choice of paradigm and of mythographic approach. Eliot, whose interest in anthropology had begun at university, knew that the comparative, universalist method employed in *The Golden Bough* only represented one possible mode of interpretation. He was fully aware of new work carried out in the area of ethnography: that is, the recording and analysis of a particular culture, including its myths and rituals, based on field research. Indeed, in the year of the publication of *The Waste Land*, there appeared also an important ethnographic work by Bronislaw Malinowksi, *Argonauts of the Western Pacific*. It was self-evidently the product of direct experience and documentation, and so ran contrary to the armchair expertise of Frazer. *Argonauts* thus focused the growing disenchantment with Frazerian comparativism, now found by many anthropologists to be too generalising, too insensitive to specific communities. But in various papers, articles and reviews in the years before *The Waste Land*, and even as late as his *Notes towards the Definition of Culture* (1948), Eliot resisted the cultural particularism of this modern 'functionalist' anthropology, as it was called. Where it referred to 'cultures' and the way they worked, he inferred from *The Golden Bough* the existence of 'culture', essential and universal. It was the unifying pattern that attracted him in Frazer's enterprise. The regrettably evolutionist proposal of an advance beyond magic and religion to science could be discarded, leaving only the idea of a global myth whose 'roots' were the basis of a collective legacy. Devoid of such a paradigm, the imaginative logic of the poem would lack its resonance. The cultural breakdown which it conveys could not be recognised as such without a basis of primitive harmony. Modernism, unlike modernity, needed its 'roots' (Manganaro 1995: 1–5).

Informed by the 'myth and ritual' school, then, *The Waste Land* is, despite appearances, a story; and the tale it tells is a deliberate fusing and updating of two other stories – that of the dying and reviving god (Frazer), and that of the quest for the Grail (Weston). Once this is realised, apparently disconnected images and incidents assume their mythic meaning; negative phenomena imply positive essences; confusion implies the need for enlightenment. However, the 'glory' of reviving god and of completed quest remains tragically elusive.

The unnamed narrator glimpses, early in the poem, a vision of beauty associated with a 'hyacinth girl' and a 'hyacinth garden'. He feels himself to be looking into 'the heart of light, the silence' (Eliot 1963: 64). In seeking to regain this vision, and to understand its meaning, he is forced to confront also Conrad's 'heart of darkness', a vision of alternating 'boredom' and 'horror'. Much of the poem takes place in the wilderness and the metropolis, each symbolising the Waste Land of modernity. The question implicitly posed is, in Frazer's perspective, what sacrifice could redeem this arid world and reaffirm the fertility cycle? In Weston's, it is a matter of whether the quester, our unnamed protagonist, can reaffirm the sacred link with the Grail and so cure the Fisher King, in a land which does not even know itself to be waste.

Taking Frazer's perspective first, we may say that the reader of the poem is left in no doubt that the fertility god has died. But the community depicted here is hardly ready for his revival. Spring brings only anxiety not rejoicing. April is 'the cruellest month' precisely because it is then that 'lilacs' emerge from 'the dead land', disturbing the habitual death-in-life of the inhabitants, winter having covered earth in 'forgetful snow'. These people may well be asked what 'roots' they know, for they are, spiritually, in a desert (Eliot 1963: 63). But they can give no answer: the 'crowds of people walking round in a ring' glimpsed by the clairvoyant Madame Sosostris are oblivious to the need for true ceremony (Eliot 1963: 64). Theirs is an empty ritual. A corpse is buried in a garden, suggesting a link with the ancient cult of Osiris, but there is no mention of any rebirth. 'Phlebas the Phoenician' drowns, sugggesting a link with the cults of both Osiris and Adonis, but the waters of death are not transformed into the waters of life (Eliot 1963: 75). As for Weston's perspective, the role of the Fisher King has been denied and degraded. Where once the fish symbolised fertility – abundant life brought out of the waters – it is now associated chiefly with desolation. The protagonist recalls fishing on a winter evening in 'the dull canal', musing upon 'the king my father's death' (Eliot 1963: 70). Again, even at the very end of the poem, the Grail monarch is still waiting to be healed, as he sits on the shore 'Fishing, with the arid plain behind me' (Eliot 1963: 79).

However, to remain with Weston's perspective, it should not escape our attention that, in the case of the phrase 'the king my father's death' (in the original, 'the King my father's wreck'), the notes refer us to *The Tempest*, the mythopoeic work of literature which we referred to in our introductory chapter, and which has much in common with Grail romance. Like Perceval, prince Ferdinand at this moment of the play (Act I, Scene 2) may be seen as on a quest: ultimately, though he does not know it, for his bride Miranda and for the inheritance of Prospero's dukedom; immediately for King Alonso, his father, whom he believes to have been drowned. No sooner has he uttered his words, however, than he hears Ariel's 'ditty'. Significantly, though the 'airy spirit' sings of death by water, he also sings of a 'sea-change/Into something rich and strange' (I. ii. 490–1). This cryptic promise will be fulfilled when Ferdinand does indeed find his father Alonso again, alive and very much changed. Again, though Eliot's quester does not discover the healing knowledge of the Grail, the symbolism is a consistent and informing presence. Further references to the legend, such as a quotation from Verlaine's poem 'Parsifal', though juxtaposed ironically with the bawdy refrain of a music-hall ballad, do remind us that in the traditional romance the king is cured. Though we have lost all assurance of that healing moment, and though we do not even hear the ritual question of the Grail, we may begin to intuit the distant beginning of some new way of life. Indeed, this is suggested, albeit desperately, by the words quoted from the Book of Isaiah: 'Shall I at least set my lands in order?' (Eliot 1963: 79).

Returning to Frazer's perspective, though the poem offers no decisive transition from dying god to reviving god, the invocation of effective sacrifice is too strong for the poem to be merely a documentation of 'boredom' and 'horror'. Though the inhabitants of the Waste Land are oblivious to the need for 'vegetation ceremonies', *The Waste Land* itself is obsessed with them. Though Madame Sosostris cannot find in her Tarot pack the card of The Hanged Man, the sign of sacrifice, the noted absence of the card has its resonance. Moreover, in both Frazer's and Weston's perspectives, the Tarot image suggests not only a 'Life Cult' but also a 'Mystery Cult', and not only a 'Mystery Cult' but also Christianity itself. Thus later in the poem, we hear of 'frosty silence in the gardens' and 'agony in stony places', of 'shouting' and 'crying' in 'Prison and palace': allusions to the crucifixion narrative. Though the inhabitants of the Waste Land can only reflect that 'He who is living is now dead', thus failing to understand that what matters about the crucifixion is the resurrection which follows it, the Gospel story is still able to be invoked to telling effect (Eliot 1963: 76).

Eliot's poem, then, while conveying 'boredom' and 'horror', gains its power from its reminder of the 'glory' which has been lost and which needs to be regained. According to Burke's thinking, this ideal is only implicit in language itself, which is 'rotten with perfection'. More particularly, it is the very nature of 'words' to suggest the one, perfect, universal 'Word' (Burke 1970: 7). And indeed, *The Waste Land*, on first sight a bewildering array of words, does insistently gesture towards some absolute, if absent, Word. By the end of the poem it has even been named: it is the Sanskrit 'Shantih', translated into Christian terms by the notes as 'The Peace which passeth understanding' (Eliot 1963: 86). Having named it, the poem invites us to lament the very distance betweeen words and Word which it enacts. It is thus that the poem itself stands as a tragic indictment of an age that seems content to leave the Word unheard. It is against the spirit of that age that the poem works: despite its demonstration of chaos, *The Waste Land* is really about the need for order. It uses the paradigm of fertility as the framework for a transcendent vision. For, no matter how lacking the age may seem in hierarchical principles and in ideas of perfection, the aesthetic ordering of words which the poem achieves is intended to stand as a reminder of the power of the all-embracing Word.

THE MYTHICAL METHOD

Eliot's quest for a saving paradigm persisted. Reviewing James Joyce's recently published novel in 1923, in an article entitled '*Ulysses*, Order and Myth', he reflected on the possibilities of 'the mythical method':

> In using the myth, in manipulating a continuous parallel between contemporaneity and antiquity, Mr Joyce is pursuing a method which others might pursue after him. They will not be imitators, any more than the scientist who uses the discoveries of Einstein in pursuing his own, independent investigations. It is simply a way of controlling, of ordering, of giving a shape and a significance to the immense panorama of futility and anarchy which is contemporary history . . . . Instead of the narrative method, we may now use the mythical method. It is, I seriously believe, a step toward making the modern world possible for art . . . . And only those who have won their own discipline in secret and without aid, in a world which offers very little assistance to that end, can be of any use in furthering this advance.
>
> (Eliot 1975: 177–8)

Before considering how far this does justice to Joyce's achievement, we might pause to note the continuity between this review and a slightly earlier, and seemingly unrelated, article. In 'Tradition and the Individual Talent' (1919) the same concepts are evident, though they are couched in slightly different terms. Thus we are told that 'tradition' involves 'aesthetic, not merely historical matters'. Only by converting historical experience into art, and then the sequence of works of art into a canon, do we become aware 'not only of the pastness of the past, but of its presence'. For the 'existing monuments' form 'an ideal order' which is modified slightly every time a fresh artefact appears and is added to it; 'and this is conformity between the old and the new.' Though this or that poem appears in time, 'tradition' is best depicted as a spatial, a 'simultaneous', arrangement of 'monuments'. Eliot implies that the effect for the contemporary reader is that of walking round what André Malraux, and after him Donald Davie, will call 'the imaginary museum'. Moreover, the task of 'the individual talent' is not to produce an 'expression' of 'emotion' and 'personality', but to attain 'impersonality'. The poet must serve 'the mind of Europe', which is 'much more important than his own private mind': 'it is a mind which . . . abandons nothing *en route*, which does not superannuate either Shakespeare, or Homer, or the rock drawing of the Magdalenian draughtsmen' (Eliot 1975: 37–44). The contemporary artist, the artist working in or around 1920, must treat as contemporary not only the author of *The Tempest* (early seventeenth century) but also the author of the *Odyssey* (eighth century BC), and must treat them both as contemporaries of the anonymous cave artists of the later palaeolithic period. For what matters is the 'simultaneous' and 'ideal order', which transcends history. That is, Eliot is using the word 'myth' in his *Ulysses* review as synonymous with the word 'tradition' in this earlier article. The fact that the common denotation is not immediately obvious only helps to render the critical rhetoric more effective. It seems only too appropriate, then, that Joyce is praised for having applied the inherited form of Homer's text to the all too diverse material of the world around him. He has, we are persuaded, managed to comprehend the chaos of modernity by utilising an ancient paradigm. That is, he has invoked the spatial, impersonal tradition rather than expressed his temporal, personal interests.

We are not to infer that Eliot has totally missed the point of Joyce's enterprise. The Homeric model is there, and the novel would not have its 'shape' without it. *Ulysses* certainly does match the *Odyssey* episode by episode; and though Eliot does not give examples, the alert reader soon recognises the parallels. Homer's text, itself loosely based on archaic hero myths, tells the following story. Odysseus, ruler of Ithaca, has been helping in the Greek army's siege of Troy. His quest is to return home and to reaffirm his identity as a man, a king and a husband. His wife Penelope is being pestered by suitors who wish her to declare herself a widow and marry one of them. His son Telemachus, believing him to be alive, sets out to find him even as he himself makes his journey. It is while Odysseus rests *en route* at the court of King Alcinous of the Phaeacians that he recounts his more marvellous adventures. These include: the encounter with the monstrous one-eyed Cyclops; the narrow escape from the charms of Circe, who can turn men into swine; the visit to Hades, or the Underworld; and the evasion of the Sirens, whose charming song can beguile sailors to their death. Eventually, Odysseus returns to Ithaca, where he is reunited with Telemachus, who has also come home. He overcomes the suitors and is restored to the bed of Penelope. Apart from using the Roman version of Odysseus' name, Ulysses, Joyce keeps assiduously close to Homer. The Cyclops becomes the aggressive, one-eyed landlord of a Dublin tavern; Circe's island becomes a modern brothel; Hades becomes an urban graveyard; the Sirens become barmaids. As for Odysseus' desire to be reunited with his son Telemachus, that is realised in the encounter towards the end of the novel between Leopold Bloom, the commercial failure, and young Stephen Daedalus, the frustrated artist. Here are two men cast adrift in the modern metropolis, finding archetypal status in their meeting, informed as it is by the Homeric context.

Eliot wants to go further than noting parallels, however. He claims that Joyce is not here merely making clever connections, but imposing an order on 'the immense panorama of futility and anarchy which is contemporary history'. In other words, 'the mythical method', made possible only by a discipline both severe and 'secret', is the necessary counterpoint to the vulgar chaos of the twentieth century. Again, we may recall parallel phrasing from 'Tradition and the Individual Talent': 'ideal order'; 'presence' of the 'past'; 'conformity between the old and the new'; 'the mind of Europe'; 'impersonality' (as opposed to 'emotion' and 'personality').

It should be obvious, then, that Eliot, in reviewing Joyce's novel, is effectively describing and commending his own poetic practice in *The Waste Land*. If for Homer we substitute the material documented by Frazer and Weston, then 'certain references to vegetation ceremonies' are what give 'a shape and a significance' to the disorder discovered. In justifying himself, he attributes to the author of *Ulysses* an affinity with his own austere principles. Whether the paradigm is heroism or fertility, it offers a means to perfection.

Two reservations have to be made, however. Firstly, Eliot uses Joyce's fiction as the opportunity to oppose 'the mythical method' to 'the narrative method'. He assumes that what matters most about *Ulysses* is the paradigm inherited from Homer rather than the actual tale it tells, the protagonist of which is a modest middle-aged Irishman and not a Greek warrior. That is, Eliot privileges form over matter, structure over story. It is as if he has forgotten what the classical Greek philosopher Aristotle (in other respects a strong influence upon him) meant when in his *Poetics* he used *mythos* in the sense of 'emplotment'. As Paul Ricoeur explains, this means 'both "fable" (in the sense of imaginary story) and "plot" (in the sense of well-constructed history)'. He adds: 'What Aristotle calls plot is not a static structure but an operation, an integrative process which . . . confers on the narrated story an identity one can call dynamic' (Ricoeur 1991: 426). It is precisely this 'dynamic' identity which Eliot overlooks, thus failing to give due weight to the dialectical nature of plot, which mediates between the temporal flow of events and the human need for hierarchy, stability, order. Eliot wants only the order, and tries to abstract the 'pure' myth informing Joyce's novel from the given sequence of events and interaction of characters. In attempting this, Eliot is treating both the *Odyssey* and *Ulysses* in the same static and externalising manner as Bultmann treats the Bible. Only, where the latter wants to separate out the doctrine from the narrative, the *kerygma* or *logos* from the Gospel *mythos*, Eliot wants to distinguish myth proper from the mere telling of tales. He takes the notion of myth as paradigm to the point of an arid formalism. The *mythos* of Homer becomes the *logos* which Joyce is credited with forcing upon his material. Thus Eliot effects his own kind of demythologization even as he proclaims the indispensability of myth; and in the process Joyce's novel is enlisted for most un-Joycean aims.

The second reservation concerns the opposition of myth and history, of 'shape and significance' and 'futility and anarchy'. Put simply, this is a simple misreading of the novel. It is as if Eliot has attributed the sentiment of Stephen Daedalus – 'History is a nightmare from which I am trying to awake' – to his creator. The most superficial acquaintance with Joyce's novel will reveal that Dublin, which indeed may be said to represent history, is very far from being chaotic. On the contrary, its network of churches and brothels, libraries and bars, may be said to cater very efficiently for the needs of its citizens. What they themselves do may border on confusion, but it would misrepresent the modern metropolis to say that it in itself embodies 'anarchy and futility'. Consider the 'Ithaca' or 'catechism' episode, in which Bloom draws water from the tap to make cocoa for himself and Stephen Daedalus at the end of their adventurous day. The water, we are told, flowed 'from Roundwood reservoir in county Wicklow of a cubic capacity of 2,400 million gallons, percolating through a subterranean aqueduct of filter mains of single and double pipeage constructed at an initial plant cost of £5 per linear yard' (Joyce 1960: 782–3). As Fredric Jameson has noted, here is order, and here is mythic power: 'the transformation of Nature by human and collective praxis' (Jameson 1982: 140–1). That is, to adapt Eliot's terms, the 'order and myth' in this chapter of *Ulysses* are focused on a revelation concerning the hidden effects of human labour, deliberately invoked by the apparent banality of the way water reaches the average Dublin house, rather than on the empty form of 'a shape and a significance' imposed from above.

The only human labour which Eliot in his review wishes to connect with myth is aesthetic. For him, 'the mythical method' is 'a step toward making the modern world possible for art'. There is his agenda in brief. 'The modern world', a world of 'futility and anarchy', is what is given. It must await 'art', identified with the 'ideal order' of 'myth', if it is to be redeemed. The possibility that human life is already structured, and already symbolic, before the artist begins his or her work, is precluded. It is as if mythopoeia, the capacity to produce myths and to provide a model of the world, belongs only to an exclusive elite. We may, of course, posit the emergence in every community of one particular 'myth man' or 'mythic specialist', to use Kenneth Burke's terms. But, as Burke insists, we misconceive this role if we take the specialisation for granted, and forget the source of its power: the general, pragmatic need to 'complete' or 'perfect' crucial events such as planting and harvesting, by way of symbolism and story (Burke 1971: 103–5).

In this elitism, which goes with his aestheticism or formalism, Eliot is a representative figure. His is the voice of a distinct, uncompromising strain in modernism. His 'mythical method' is one way, one extreme way, of expressing an urge which a poem by his contemporary Wallace Stevens presents paradoxically as the 'blessed rage for order'. By contrasting the ways in which Stevens and Eliot exemplify this 'rage', we might manage, provisionally, to place the latter's mythic interests. In his poem, 'The Idea of Order at Key West', Stevens begins by contrasting the uncompromising force of the sea with the fragile power of a woman's song. By the end he has demonstrated that, if we need the sea, or reality, for the imagination to work upon, then so does the sea find meaning in the human ability to 'sing', to produce art (Stevens 1986: 65–6). This might be seen as an anticipation of what in physics has come to be called 'the anthropic principle': human consciousness is in some mysterious way fitted to the universe, and vice versa. It might also be seen as a reaffirmation of a theme in Romantic poetry. After all, Wordsworth and Coleridge made the relationship between reality and imagination the very subject of their verse. In *The Prelude* and 'Kubla Khan', in odes such as 'Intimations of Immortality' and 'Dejection', they sought to vindicate the ideal of poetry as illumination rather than mere reflection, and the poet as visionary rather than scribe. Stevens in 'Key West' is perhaps benefiting from this legacy, and within the poem endorsing their faith. In his whole body of work, he seeks to construct 'the Supreme Fiction', the synthesis of reality and imagination in one great symbolic narrative. Never to be completed, and important mainly for its celebration of the very world we inhabit, this provisional, human myth is to be believed in where most it contradicts dead doctrines and rigid hierarchies. For 'the great poems of heaven and hell have been written and the great poem of the earth remains to be written' (Stevens 1984: 142).

But though 'rage for order' may describe Eliot's own poetic effort, his 'mythical method' is meant to be a programme as far as possible from that of 'the visionary company' (to use Hart Crane's phrase). It seems to involve little trust in that ultimate accord of the world and the soul which Coleridge sought to espouse, despite all doubts, in his 'Dejection' ode: 'we receive but what we give'; and 'in our life alone does Nature live' (Coleridge 1971: 106). This dialectic of imagination and reality is not Eliot's business. His 'ideal order' invokes the classical tradition, or at least one austere version of it, rather than the Romantic. In his 'neo-classicism', nature is to be revered only in so far as it is formalised, and no harmony is to be anticipated from the interaction propounded by Coleridge. This order underpins his distinct complex of conservatism, pronounced by himself on the occasion of his conversion to Christianity in 1928 in the following words: 'classicist in literature, royalist in politics, and anglo-catholic in religion' (Eliot 1970: 7). Here an extreme form of what Burke calls 'perfectionism' is made explicit: for Eliot, art and history alike demand fulfilment in hierarchy; words demand fulfilment in the Word. The paradigm of fertility has led him to his own exclusive vision of perfection.

2

CHAOS

THE COMIC VISION

Having identified the paradigm on which Eliot deliberately based his particular idea of perfection, and indicated how he moved from the story of the dying god to the formulation of an aesthetic, political and religious doctrine, we will perhaps be entitled to some scepticism about his claim to represent universal order. We might feel entitled to replace his phrase 'the mythical method' with the more accurate one, 'a mythical method'. Modernism did not produce just one distinct brand of mythopoeia. Here we will contrast Eliot's tragic vision with the comic vision of a poet and critic who consciously defined his own enterprise against that of Eliot – namely Edgell Rickword.

Perhaps we might situate this contrast by citing Kenneth Burke again. In his 'Definition of Man' he reminds us of Aristotle's designation of the human being as 'the laughing animal'. Burke goes further: 'mankind's only hope is a cult of comedy'. For: 'The cult of tragedy is too eager to help out with the holocaust. And in the last analysis, it is too pretentious to allow for the proper recognition of our animality' (Burke 1966: 20). Cryptic as these observations are, they may offer a clue to why Rickword set himself the task of exposing what he saw as Eliot's reactionary elitism. Two kinds of modernism, and two understandings of myth, were involved.

When Eliot founded his long-running journal, *The Criterion* (1922–39), he did so, as his editorials constantly reminded his readers, to defend a classical ideal of 'reason'. In this endeavour he was frequently challenged by a short-lived rival magazine, *The Calendar of Modern Letters* (1925–7), which persistently referred to Eliot's 'reason' as just another word for 'repression'. It accused him of adopting a defensive aesthetic position, which was the complement of a 'reactionary' political and theological position. The journal's main editor was the English poet and critic, Edgell Rickword. He was also the author of *Rimbaud: The Boy and the Poet* (1924), which was the first critical biography of the rebellious Symbolist published in English. Two years after '*Ulysses*, Order and Myth' appeared, *The Calendar* printed his own essay 'The Returning Hero'. There would seem to have been a connection, in that the project advocated by Rickword almost wilfully contradicts that of Eliot. 'A Hero would seem to be due', he declares, an 'exhaustively disillusioned' one 'who has yet so much vitality' as to create 'an unbiased but self-consistent, humorous universe':

> Possibly he will be preceded (I should say that he is being preceded) by some tumbling, flour-faced harbingers to the progress (for we cannot grow serious all at once) just as the death-defying wire-walker in the circus is led into the ring by clowns who mime his tragedy. Perhaps the Hero will be one of those loons himself, for the death-defying gesture is a demoded luxury in the modern State. So long as the social mind has no coherent expression like that given it by a supernatural explanation of the universe, the fantastic and the comic, disintegrating forces, will continue the most reputable of styles. They

need by no means be inimical to heroic poetry, to which not dignity is essential, but a conception of power.

(Rickword 1974: 118)

Rickword adds that the further this new kind of hero myth can be removed from 'conventional erotic, ethical, or other social values' the better, for then it will regain the strength of 'the old culture'. By this term he seems to refer to the repressed 'folk' imagination, the source of all mythic paradigms. Thus where Eliot's 'mythical method' would impose a strict form on 'futility and anarchy', would answer vulgar chaos with classical convention, Rickword's new hero would trust to a residual mythopoeic urge. In doing so, he would spontaneously move the age beyond defeat and depression.

The mythic paradigm which is the starting point for Eliot is that of fertility, and from there he proceeds to consider also the hero myth (in his review of *Ulysses*). The mythic paradigm which is the starting point for Rickword is the hero myth, which he takes to imply the cyclical model of fertility (with his very notion of a 'returning' hero). But perhaps the difference between the two could be stated even more simply. For Eliot myth connotes tragic restraint; for Rickword it connotes comic release.

After all, *The Golden Bough* depicts fertility magic as conducted between two poles: that of the dying god and that of the reviving god. *The Waste Land* may be said to keep quite close to the lower pole: while the fertility paradigm serves as the basis for a hierarchical vision, the poem itself is primarily a lament for the spiritual emptiness of an age. The distance of words from Word is dramatised as a collective tragedy. History is viewed as 'an immense panorama of futility and anarchy'. This is a legitimate theme for poetry, and one representative of much modernist work. But Eliot errs when he seeks to enlist the author of *Ulysses* into his own cause. Joyce really belongs to that other modernist stratagem, the case for which is given by Rickword in 'The Returning Hero'.

The possibility is not only that the god may revive, but that his revival may be 'comic' in terms both of structure and mood. That is, firstly, if his business is not 'dignity' but 'power', then the crucial issue is whether he revives, whether he moves from death to life: a matter of structure. And secondly, if 'power' is not what we normally mean, but is rather associated with the force of human laughter, then his new life will be the source not of a solemn order but of infinite revelry: a matter of mood. Moreover, whereas Eliot thinks the important thing about *Ulysses* is the supposedly pure, abstract shape of hero myth underlying the *Odyssey*, Rickword's 'Hero' would seem to confound all paradigms. That is, he has the centrality of a reviving god, but he has the sense of absurdity of a laughing animal. For above all, his universe will be 'humorous'; and he himself will emerge from the ranks of 'clowns' or 'loons'. He is, then, a force for endlessly productive imperfection rather than for arid and static perfection.

Leopold Bloom, in so far as he is a mock-hero, anticipates this conception. But it is in *Finnegans Wake* (1939) that Joyce realises the possibility most clearly. Unlike Eliot's vision, Joyce's is democratically undignified and droll. Thus H.C.E. is announced as 'our low hero': 'O! the lowness of him was beneath all up to that sunk to!' And yet he is Joyce's very device for comprehending 'All marryvoising moodmoulded cyclewheeling history'. *Finnegans Wake* is a 'gaiety pantheomime' ('pan-theo-mime', the dance of the gods, identifed with the whole of nature). It takes the reader to 'The poignt of fun where I am crying to arrive you at': that is, the moment where tragedy is understood to be only an aspect of comedy (Joyce 1966: 171, 186). Thus Norman O. Brown praises the principle of 'Finnegan Beginnagain', which takes us back beyond the tragic to 'something more elemental' (Brown 1973: 60). Even those who have not attempted to read Joyce's last novel may know that it is over 600 pages long, and that it begins halfway through the sentence which breaks off, requiring completion by the reader, on the last page. It is massively cyclical, comprehensively comic, 'disintegrating' habitual discourse (as Rickword would have it) but thereby offering 'the social mind' a new sense of 'power' by demanding an effort of return and renewal. According to Umberto Eco, it is a profoundly paradoxical book in that it assumes both order and disorder simultaneously: it constitutes a 'Chaosmos', a mixture of cosmos and chaos, which might be said to facilitate a new mode of living for this and the next century (Eco 1989: 87).

The Calendar was unqualified in its praise of Joyce, and recognised him as an essentially comic writer. As for Rickword's own writing, we might see the logic of 'The Returning Hero' at work by glancing over one of his volumes of poetry, namely *Invocations to Angels* (1928). In 'To the Sun and Another Dancer' he takes Weston's hypothesis that Christianity is a mystery cult deriving from fertility religion and, rewriting the Easter story in terms of the mating of male sun and female earth, produces his own mythically structured love poem. Again, though the parodic 'masque', 'A Happy New Year', is clearly derived from *The Golden Bough*, it avoids the earnestness of Eliot's investment in that work. With dances performed by 'The Frazer Eight' and 'The Lebanon Girls', it suggests a scepticism about that source even while it acknowledges the validity of the fertility paradigm. Thus 'A Happy New Year' is both like and unlike *The Waste Land*. It is like it in that, as the 'Girls' mime the death of the god, his rebirth stands in the balance: their 'little pot-clay Edens, mimic groves/of fresh-plucked twigs that symbolise desire' are 'swift-withering on the edge of expectation' (Rickword 1976: 82–3). It is unlike *The Waste Land* in that Rickword does not associate the paradigm of fertility with aesthetic and cosmic order, but with human possibility. The god is seen as a 'heavenly Ploughman', whose task is 'to draw Time's toppling wain/to all-men's Harvest Home'. Thus the masque concludes with the presenter having a vision of 'others who walk the earth tonight', secular 'pilgrims' passing through a desolate city, making their way 'to a lucid zone, whence fresh horizons blazed' (Rickword 1976: 86). There is a way out of the Waste Land, but it need not be Eliot's. Here the horizon of possibility replaces the hierarchy of perfection. Indeed, the 'others' who chart the way might well be those figures excluded or patronised by his ascetic 'mythical method'. In another poem, 'Terminology', Rickword offers his vision of what Ricoeur calls an 'unprecedented' world. He imagines a moment, inconceivable in Eliot's context, when 'women grown/too docile under habits not their own' and 'all tense lives' which have been 'subdued to what they seem' will 'stand up unsullied' in 'Time's stream' (Rickword 1976: 41).

One line from this last poem, in which Rickword compares the oppressed women to 'shirted angels nailed to bedroom walls', is reminiscent of the vivid, hallucinatory verse of Arthur Rimbaud. In his study of that poet, Rickword praises the 'visionary' for having 'rebelled against the gods of order and tradition':

> if his art could function only at the expense of some confusion or distortion, there must be some great difference between his art and what we call art. And there was, for with us art is the setting of limits where psychologically there are no limits. Rimbaud desired his art to disregard even this capital condition, even though chaos were the price.
>
> (Rickword 1974: 118, 157)

For Rickword, the paradox of Rimbaud's work is that, while offering us a glimpse into chaos, or *Season in Hell* (as one of his works is entitled), it is 'often more serenely classic than that of any other modern' (Rickword 1974: 112). In the next section, we will consider another poet who was prepared to forego any received discipline, and plunge headlong into chaos.

SINGER AS SHAMAN

On 15 May 1871 Rimbaud wrote a letter to his friend Paul Demeny, which Rickword translates in *Rimbaud: The Boy and the Poet*:

> The poet makes himself a *visionary* by a long immense and reasoned *derangement* of *all the senses*. . . . For he comes to the *unknown*! . . . Though he collapses in his leaping among things unheard-of and nameless, other horrific labourers will come; they will begin at the horizons where the other sank.
>
> (Rickword 1974: 126)

Wallace Fowlie has well documented the influence which the writer of those words had on the poet and lead singer of The Doors, Jim Morrison (Fowlie 1994: 121–30). Morrison clearly saw himself as a visionary, and was certainly prepared to undergo a derangement of the senses in acting out the role. More importantly for us, he followed Rimbaud in seeking both to write and to live mythically, in defiance of convention. Like Rickword's 'returning Hero', he did not mind appearing as a 'loon', nor summoning up 'disintegrating forces' and defying 'conventional erotic, ethical, or other social values', in order to forge a new 'conception of power'.

In his poem 'An American Prayer', Morrison seeks to realise this new mythic awareness and challenge the logic of modern rationality, which culminates in war. He calls for us to 'reinvent the gods, all the myths of the ages', in order to counter the 'fat slow generals' who are 'getting obscene on young blood' (Morrison 1991: 3). Figuring himself as lizard, reptile, snake, Morrison affects to have achieved the wisdom of the *ourobos*, the symbolic snake that continually renews its own life by eating its own tail. As 'lizard king' he further affects to be provoking humanity out of its present state of torpor; but paradoxically this means he is really leading them backward, to the moment of origin, so that they may be cured of the disease of linear history – the story of 'the American night'. The paradigm here is fertility myth; but, as we shall see, for Morrison this structure overlaps with that of creation myth.

Describing the impact and import of The Doors in 1967, Jim Morrison invoked the power of ritual. He saw America in need of rebirth: that is, redemption from the narrow, bureaucratic rationality that led to Vietnam and to global pollution. The only way to counter this shallow logic of progress was to recover the wisdom of archaic ceremony:

> First you have to have the period of disorder, chaos, returning to a primeval disaster region. Out of that you purify the elements and find a new seed of life, which transforms all life and all matter and the personality until finally, hopefully, you emerge and marry all those dualisms and opposites. Then you're not talking about evil and good anymore but something unified and pure. Our music and personalities are still in a state of chaos and disorder with maybe an incipient element of purity kind of starting.
>
> (Hopkins and Sugerman 1980: 143)

Conceiving of his art as a 'purification ritual', taking himself and his followers, or fans, through disorder and chaos to 'some cleaner, freer realm', Morrison here identifies with the medieval alchemist. But more usually, his authority is referred to the archaic role of the 'shaman': that is, 'priest or witch-doctor of class claiming to have sole contact with gods etc' (*OED*). This is perhaps the most productive analogy by which to characterise his poetic performance, which he grandly refers to as 'the ceremony'.

Frazer explicitly linked the shaman with the King of the Wood, in turn identified with the all-powerful magician. Morrison himself explicitly aligns himself with this power in the internal commentary of 'The Lords'. But in doing so he shows his dissatisfaction with the fertility paradigm, as interpreted and effectively tamed by Frazer. The shaman achieved 'a sensuous panic, deliberately evoked through drugs, chants, dancing'. Shamans were 'professional hysterics' who 'were once esteemed'. Indeed: 'They mediated between man and spirit-world. Their mental travels formed the crux of the religious life of the tribe' (Morrison 1985: 24). Taking Morrison's point, we may add that the important thing about the shaman is that, in contrast to a conventional priest, he is not instructed in a body of doctrine; rather, he acquires his own powers. There is no *logos*, no fixed scheme or formula, for him to hold onto: he has to trust to the *mythos*, the narrative process of psychic exploration. Only by transcending all definitions, whether of god or of self, can transformation take place. Orthodox beliefs and systems have to be left behind, and one must proceed by the sheer force of imagination. Only thus may temporality and totality coincide, and time be turned into eternity.

Though *The Golden Bough* may be a reference point for Morrison, his enthusiasm for the role of shaman must be radically distinguished from the rationalist calm of Frazer's documentation. Situating the singer, we have to forget modernity, with its myth of mythlessness, represented by Frazer's conviction that humanity could and should progress beyond magic and religion. As we shall see, we have also to distinguish the impulse described above from that of modernism, as represented by Eliot's poetic appropriation of Frazer's material. Morrison is best understood as representing what Hans Bertens calls the 'postmodernism of immediacy and presence', expressed most effectively in 'performance art' (Bertens 1995: 74). Interestingly, the authority Bertens cites for this concept is an expert on shamanism. Suzi Gablik describes a process in which 'the artist as shaman' becomes 'a conductor of forces', who is able 'to bring art back in touch with its sacred sources'. That is, 'through his own personal self-transformation, he develops not only new forms of art, but new forms of living'. For Gablik, the new shaman is a 'mystical, priestly, and political figure' who has become a 'visonary and a healer' (Bertens 1995: 74–5).

Morrison's art may fairly be described, then, as postmodernist, pop neo-shamanism. But if we ignore the second epithet, then we miss the point. Rock-'n'-roll, with its amplified music and universal appeal, has mythic potential in its own right, if we are to believe the late Marshall McLuhan: 'Electric circuitry confers a mythic dimension on our ordinary individual and group actions. Our technology forces us to live mythically, but we continue to think fragmentarily, and on single, separate planes' (McLuhan 1967: 114). In *The Medium is the Message*, we learn that the electronic age in general, and pop music in particular, enables us to prove anew the immediacy and simultaneity of experience apparently enjoyed by our pre-literate ancestors. According to the anthropologist Lévy-Bruhl (1857–1939) the archaic mind enjoyed a capacity for 'mystical participation', of individual with group and of group with cosmos. This capacity was lost with the advance of civilisation and literacy. But McLuhan's account of popular culture suggests that the new oral-electronic age allows humans to integrate and intensify their lives again.

As a poet seeking to render his poetry accessible to the new pop audience of the post-war years, Jim Morrison might be seen as embodying the major shift in sensibility discerned by McLuhan. He would certainly count as one of those who restores the vitality of pre-literate culture by making poetry radically popular once more. In his hands the poem becomes an inclusive performance rather than an exclusive artefact. In McLuhan's perspective, to listen to a Doors record or attend a Doors concert is to participate in a new collectivity. The only ones excluded from this are those still living in 'the Gutenberg galaxy', where a poem is not a song, an overwhelming experience, but an arid series of words on a page. And, if we are to take the full force of the statements quoted above, Morrison may be envisaged as a myth-maker in the sense of offering a means to Lévy-Bruhl's 'mystical participation'; or, in McLuhan's formulation, giving 'young people' the very 'formula for putting on the universe' which they are looking for (McLuhan 1967: 114).

McLuhan's echo of Lévy-Bruhl's hypothesis of a pre-modern, anti-rational, non-positivist mentality raises the question of what model of myth is at work here. Lévy-Bruhl set himself against Frazer, whom he took to be unsympathetic to primitive thinking and fearful of the excesses of the mythopoeic imagination. Moreover, Frazer's seasonal pattern of death and revival failed to do justice to the intuition of cosmic forces that Lévy-Bruhl saw as crucial to myth. As Brian Morris points out, the significance of this kind of mythography was that, rejecting the Frazerian notion of myth as an intellectual error to be exposed by objective means, it fostered an interest in myth as a symbolic and subjective expression (Morris 1987: 182). But, though it obviously helps us situate Morrison, we have yet to clarify his choice of paradigm. Here we should acknowledge briefly his undoubted debt to the Romantic poet William Blake, who will be discussed further in Part II. He is the source of the name of Morrison's band: 'If the doors of perception were cleansed, everything would appear to man as it is, infinite' (Blake 1971: 154). Certainly, Morrison's lyrics are all about seeing beyond the obsessively normative rationality of the contemporary American mind, beyond what Blake called 'single vision': 'Break on through to the other side' (Doors 1992: 10). But what, mythically, do these words mean? Here we need to spell out the influence of the German philosopher, Friedrich Nietzsche (1844–1900), who developed the complementary myths of 'eternal recurrence' and 'the superman'.

Put starkly, the former is the story by which the protagonist of the latter saves himself. In affirming his own existence to the point where he happily wills that his whole life might be repeated again and again forever, the superman becomes divine:

What if a demon crept after you one day or night in your loneliest solitude and said to you: 'This life, as you live it now and have lived it, you will have to live again and again, times without number; and there will be nothing new in it, but every

pain and every joy and every thought and sigh and all the
unspeakably small and great in your life must return to you, and
everything in the same sequence – and in the same way this
spider and this moonlight among the trees, and in the same
way this moment and I myself. The eternal hour-glass of existence will be turned again and again – and you with it, you dust
of dust!' – Would you not throw yourself down and gnash
your teeth and curse the demon who thus spoke? Or have you
experienced a tremendous moment in which you would have
answered him: 'You are a god and never did I hear anything
more divine!'

(Nietzsche 1977: 249–50)

What we have here, then, is the fertility paradigm translated
simultaneously into the terms of the creation and hero paradigms.
The fertility paradigm gives us the idea of human life as cyclical.
The creation paradigm gives us the idea of facing up to primordial
chaos, manifest in the absurdity of repetition, and so beginning
life anew, as if from the very moment in which the universe
began. The hero paradigm gives us the possibility of a human
protagonist acting with a superhuman power: in this case, the
power to live without regret. Indeed, if we are prepared to say 'yes'
to life in this context of absurd, cyclical repetition, we are no
longer living as mere human beings but have ourselves become
gods. Or rather, the gods have ceased to dwell in the heights
of Olympus; they have been rendered thoroughly material,
thoroughly human. If for the shaman time becomes eternity, for
the superman eternity becomes time.

So deification consists in our being able to will that whatever is,
shall be: it is the love of fate. Dionysus, dismembered by the
Titans, to be born again from Zeus' thigh, and subsequently
glorified as the god of ecstasy and transformation, replaces the
figure of Christendom, 'the Crucified'. The latter is a curse *on* life,
pointing to a redemption *from* life. The former, though torn to

pieces, is a promise *of* life, teaching us how to live *in* life – eternally reborn without any ascetic doctrine, whether metaphysical or moral. Morrison too rejects the Christian way, understood as life-negation: 'Cancel my subscription to the resurrection', he declares in 'When the Music's Over' (Doors 1992: 32). A contemporary Dionysus, Morrison is also Rimbaud's 'visionary': the life is as mythic as the art, and the truly heroic narrative is the rejection of the given paradigm, hierarchy and perfection. Hence 'We Could Be So Good Together' (*Waiting for the Sun*, 1968) foretells a world 'without lament', one of endless, recurrent 'invitation and invention' (Doors 1992: 40). The hero myth overlaps with the creation myth, and a new cosmos is envisaged as proceeding from a new kind of hero–poet who is prepared to pay the price of chaos.

The principle of 'Chaosmos' is evident in Morrison's most famous work, the song which Coppola uses for the soundtrack of *Apocalypse Now*: 'The End'. Richard Goldstein, in his review of The Doors' first album proclaims this work as 'Joycean pop'. That is right, and it would have been wrong had he said 'Eliotean'. However, to appreciate this last point, we have first to acknowledge the main similarity between 'The End' and *The Waste Land*. As with Eliot's poem, the primitive and the sophisticated, the simple and the complex, the antique and the new, are apprehended together, and are allowed to comment one on the other. Thus we are 'Lost in a *Roman* wilderness of pain' (my emphasis): this takes us back to the curious custom of Nemi, noted by Frazer as having survived into classical civilisation, standing even then as a reminder of the Roman empire's 'savage' past. It also reminds us of what happened to Rome: how it declined into barbarism through its decades of 'pain' – of persecution, torture, sadism. Are the United States by implication identified with this decadence? We do not need to be told, perhaps, and we move on, or rather back, to the source of Frazer's primitive fertility religion. In their 'desperate land', the Waste Land, the people are 'Waiting for the summer rain', and are 'desperately in need of some stranger's hand'. The old King of the Wood is dead, but has not been replaced by the new, because we cannot remember the ritual significance of renewal. Meanwhile we are spiritually desolate, as connoted by 'All the children are insane'. What is the answer? It is twofold: 'Ride the king's highway' (follow the way of the god) and 'Ride the snake' to 'The ancient lake' (trust to fertility, mystery, sexuality). But the song ends in uncertainty: inviting us 'to picture what will be,/So limitless and free', yet concluding with the refrain, 'This is the end'. Whether the end leads to a new beginning is left unclear. The call of the shaman is not easy to follow, especially not in unpropitious times.

Accompanying this narrative of collective trauma, there is in 'The End' another story, and another trauma: that of the re-enactment of the Oedipus myth. In this the son announces to the father: 'I want to kill you' (Doors 1992: 19). We must defer discussion of the Oedipal complex, but here we may note Morrison's perceptiveness in seeing the hidden link between Freud and Frazer. The child who fantasises about killing his father and marrying his mother, and so repeating the offence of Oedipus, is here economically aligned with the runaway slave who wishes to replace the reigning King of the Wood at Nemi. By juxtaposing the two stories, he intensifies the sexual content of Frazer's material and the mythic content of Freud's psycho-analysis. After all, the 'snake' of the earlier part of the song is an ambiguous image, at once phallus and seasonal cycle, sexuality and cosmic wisdom. Moreover, the injunction, 'Ride the snake', is as much playful as it is portentous.

Having acknowledged that irony and ambiguity characterise both *The Waste Land* and 'The End', we should stress that the latter works by way of the ritual urgency of rock-'n'-roll rather than the elitist allusion of modernism. Not so much a 'rage for order' as a rage for purifying disorder, Morrison's mythopoeia is that of Rickword's and Joyce's carnivalesque heroes rather than Eliot's world-weary persona (partially identified in his own notes to the poem as Tiresias, the old, blind seer of Greek legend). More generally, the summons to 'break on through to the other side', which recurs in various forms throughout Morrison's oeuvre, is opposed to high modernism in two respects. Firstly, it is subversive in so far as it impels and organises alternative forms of solidarity ('the other side' as the counter-culture). Secondly, and more importantly for Morrison himself, it signifies the possibility of a spiritual renewal (access to 'the other side') which does not deny, but rather transforms, the life of the body. Eliot in 'Tradition and the Individual Talent' defined poetry as an 'escape from emotion' (Eliot 1975: 43). The Doors explore and expand emotion to the point of Dionysian affirmation.

THE SACRED AND THE PROFANE

Morrison, we have said, saw himself as able to reach 'the other side' because he had assumed the role of neo-shaman. A world authority on shamanism was Mircea Eliade, a Romanian scholar who became, and remained until his recent death, chairman of the department of history of religion at the University of Chicago. His expertise was the 'phenomenology' of religious experience: that is, what it feels like to be *homo religiosus* or 'the religious human'. He affirmed shamanism to be the practice providing the key to primitive humanity's attempt to live *in illo tempore* – 'in those times' or 'once upon a time'. By association, he saw all myth and ritual as an attempt to start the world again, as it was in the beginning, before the fall into mundane experience:

> In this respect, the mystical experience of primitives is equivalent to a *journey back to the origins*, a regression into the mythical time of the Paradise lost. For the shaman in ecstasy, this present world, our fallen world – which, according to modern terminology, is under the laws of Time and History – is done away with.

> (Eliade 1968: 64)

Morrison would seem to have gained his understanding of shamanism from Frazer. But it is perhaps Eliade who has the better grasp of the subject, and who provides the more relevant theoretical context for understanding The Doors' achievement. There again we have to be clear from the start that Eliade, as a general mythographer, weighs his evidence as deliberately as Frazer in order to favour his chosen paradigm. For Frazer, it is fertility which is the key to myth; for Eliade, it is creation.

Eliade has an advantage in this respect, if we consider the pre-historic evidence. To assume that fertility ritual is the source of myth and religion is to ignore the fact that such a ritual could not have started until the invention of agriculture in the neolithic period or New Stone Age – in about 8000 BC. Eliade infers that there must have been myth and ritual before then, in the later stages of the palaeolithic period or Old Stone Age – perhaps as early as about 40,000 BC. (There is indeed evidence of religious ceremony and art from about this time, as Eliot himself indicated by his allusion to 'the rock drawing of the Magdalenian draughtsmen' in 'Tradition and the Individual Talent'.) This early, pre-agricultural culture could hardly have been concerned with the seasonal cycle of the crops, since its economy was that of hunter-gathering. Eliade's assumption is that the first myth must have been creation myth. The archaic mind knew that, for the world to be lived in, it had first to be founded: hence the essential narrative would have been one of creation and not of fertility.

This may seem a matter of anthropological rather than literary debate, but poets such as Eliot and Morrison need to be understood in this context. Eliade is saying that the primary mythic logic worked as follows. Firstly, there must have been the moment of creation, which took place in 'sacred time'. Secondly, given that humanity knew that event to have taken place in the distant past, it felt itself to have fallen into 'profane time'. Whatever ceremonies archaic (that is, palaeolithic) humans performed, whatever stories they told, they were attempting to turn 'profane' back into 'sacred time'. On the one hand, the very distinction reminds us of Eliot's opposition between myth and history, between 'order' and 'futility and anarchy'. On the other hand, there is an implicit justification for Morrison's belief that paradise may be regained by pushing the fallen imagination to the point where it may 'break on through to the other side'. For Eliade is keen to demonstrate what he calls 'the dialectic of the sacred':

> The sacred is qualitatively different from the profane, yet it may manifest itself no matter how or where in the profane world because of its power of turning any natural object into a paradox by means of a hierophany [i.e. manifestation of the sacred].
>
> (Eliade 1958: 30)

To gain the full benefits of this approach to myth, however, we need to push it further. Fortunately, Thomas Altizer in his study of Eliade has demonstrated the potential of the phrase, 'dialectic of the sacred', by expanding it to include its implicit term. He speaks of 'the dialectic of the sacred and the profane'. That is, the ideal of the sacred is generated by the reality of the profane. Without the feeling of having fallen, paradise would not make sense. Without the experience of profane time there could be no conception of sacred time. Ultimately – though we should again stress that it needs Altizer, a Christian theologian, to spell out what is left unstated by Eliade – the very dialectic of sacred and profane produces the discovery of a 'coincidence of opposites', by which the sacred is apprehended anew out of, and in tension with, the profane. Indeed, reading Eliade in the light of Altizer leaves us in no doubt about the function of myth and ritual. Myth is the language within which archaic humanity narrates its awareness of the discrepancy between sacred time and profane time, and in which it projects their reconciliation. Ritual is the means by which it seeks to translate the mere chronology of profane time into the coincidence of sacred and profane. If all goes well, as it does instinctively in the shamanic trance, *this* time can become the moment in which 'cosmos' first emerged from 'chaos': the ritual transports us back to the crucial, creative moment. It enacts the dialectic of chaos and cosmos. Moreover, the mythic/ritual sense is that which knows the merely individual as the archetypal, and ordinary things as 'hierophanies'. One tree becomes 'the Tree of the World', one pool or lake becomes 'the Primordial Waters': a transcendent space is carved out of a fallen world of banality and habit, just as eternity is re-formed out of temporal existence.

Another way of putting the latter process is that renewal *in* time turns out to be renewal *of* time. Primitive humanity 'lives in a continual present'. For 'the life of archaic man', though it takes place in time, 'does not bear the burden of time' (Eliade 1971: 86). 'Myth' is, then, synonymous with 'eternal return', with the desire to be at one with a cosmic beginning in 'a continual present', an eternal now. Thus, for example, in the Babylonian new year festival, or *akitu*, the moment when chaos had originally become cosmos was lived through again, as if it were actually happening there and then. The combat between the young warrior god Marduk and the primal sea-monster Tiamat was re-enacted by two groups of actors, struggling against one another; the myth of creation, known as 'Enuma elish' (from its opening phrase, 'When on high . . . ') was recited. 'The mythical event was present: "May he continue to conquer Tiamat and shorten her days!" the celebrant exclaimed. The combat, the victory, and the Creation took place *at that very moment*' (Eliade 1971: 56).

Eliade's celebration of creation myth and ritual as the re-affirmation of order and as the achievement of presence may suggest an affinity with Eliot's use of Frazer's account of fertility myth and ritual. Apart from the obvious difference in choice of paradigm, the affinity is striking. It must, then, be recognised, but it needs qualifying. Both Eliot and Eliade are interested in the question of 'form'; and both see this as an originary and universal pattern, which humanity needs to regain. However, the 'mythical method', while it seems to involve treating antique narrative paradigms as if active in the present, is really a means of opposing sacred order to profane experience; whereas implicit in the notion of 'hierophany' is the necessity, indeed primacy, of the latter. After all, there can be no 'Tree of the World' until the archaic mind singles out this or that actual tree as specially symbolic. Moreover, Eliot associates form with the higher discipline of Western art or Eastern philosophy; for Eliade it is an aboriginal impulse, which has all too often been obscured by sophisticated speculation:

> Any form whatever, by the mere fact that it exists as such and endures, necessarily loses vigour and becomes worn; to recover vigour, it must be reabsorbed into the formless if only for an instant; it must be restored to the primordial unity from which it issued; in other words, it must return to 'chaos' (on the cosmic plane) to 'orgy' (on the social plane), to 'darkness' (for seed), to 'water' (baptism on the human plane, Atlantis on the plane of history, and so on).
>
> (Eliade 1971: 88)

It is by reaffirming form, that is the 'archetype' or primordially creative image, through the very act of returning to chaos, that archaic humanity is cured of the fall from paradise. It is in this respect that Eliade helps us appreciate Morrison's art and conduct, extravagant and indulgent as they may seem. For neo-shamanism is an attempt to push the experience of the profane to its limits, until a new sense of the sacred becomes possible. The only way is to 'break on through to the other side'.

That said, it would be misleading to conclude our account of Eliade by leaving the impression that his mythography is designed to condone counter-cultural rock music. For his acknowledgement of archaic humanity's need periodically to return to chaos, if necessary by means of orgy, should not distract us from his ultimate aim, which is the defence of an absolutist model of mythology. That is, his choice of the creation paradigm to the exclusion of all others allows him to promote a pure ideal of sacred origin, which he takes to be essentially and eternally valid. For we must be clear that Eliade, no less than Eliot, is advocating his own model of transcendence. Thus: 'The fact that a hierophany is always a historical event (that is to say, always occurs in some definite situation) does not lessen its universal quality' (Eliade 1958: 3). Indeed, the historical manifestation, subject as it is to variation and deterioration, cannot alter that quality. Once the archaic mind has constructed myths and rituals which suggest the existence of a primal time and place, these acquire total independence. As the years pass, and people forget their purpose, they continue to exist regardless of whether they elicit any human response: 'For a symbolism does not depend upon being understood; it remains consistent in spite of every corruption and preserves its structure even when it has long been forgotten, as witness those pre-historic symbols whose meaning is lost for thousands of years to be "rediscovered" later' (Eliade 1958: 450). As Robert Segal has argued, this is to assert religion as something opposed to, or at best indifferent to, the human act of belief. If Eliade is saying that a sacred entity retains its meaning even when nobody recognises it, whether consciously or unconsciously, which it appears he does, then he effectively 'separates religion from believers' (Segal 1992: 147). This position is Burke's 'perfectionism' taken to the point of absurdity, or at least self-contradiction. Eliade's documentation of myth and ritual indicates that they are the means by which human beings construct a sense of cosmic harmony, persuading themselves that they live *in illo tempore*; but simultaneously Eliade wants to argue that myth and ritual are 'completed' or 'perfected' only by acquiring a hierarchical status independent of human endeavour. In short, myth and ritual not only help humans transcend history but themselves transcend history. Thus the concession that the sacred and the profane exist dialectically, that sacred time is only conceivable given the experience of having fallen into profane time, would seem to be incidental to Eliade's main aim, which is to reserve a large stock of the sacred free from human and historical taint. In that respect, Eliade is an ally of Eliot rather than Morrison.

THE HEART-OF-DARKNESS TRIP

If, despite our doubts about Eliade, we can still take away from our preceding discussion a sense of the complementary nature of chaos and cosmos, we might briefly consider in that light another text which has associations with *Apocalypse Now*. Michael Herr, the scriptwriter for Willard's narration in Coppola's film, is also the author of an account of his own reporting of the Vietnam war for *Rolling Stone* magazine, grimly entitled *Dispatches*. This work is particularly interesting because its very subject is the challenge to make sense out of apparently senseless experience. As such it might be read as a postmodernist hero myth, in which the hero's task is not to slay a dragon but to face the full horror and absurdity of postmodern warfare without surrendering entirely the notion of some hypothetical order.

Early in the book, a GI offers to tell Herr a 'story': 'Patrol went up the mountain. One man came back. He died before he could tell us what happened.' Herr waits for the rest, 'but it seemed not to be that kind of story' (Herr 1978: 14). The subject of *Dispatches* itself might be described as the attempt to decide what kind of story one may tell about Vietnam, given its horrific chaos. The disorder is enacted by the prose: 'your vision blurring, images jumping and falling as though they were being received by a dropped camera, hearing a hundred horrible sounds at once – screams, sobs, hysterical shouting, a throbbing inside your head that threatened to take over, quavering voices trying to get the orders out, the dulls and sharps of weapons going off' (Herr 1978: 170). But there is perhaps an implicit order, in the book's first and last chapter titles: 'Breathing In' and 'Breathing Out'. The paradigm suggested is the hero's descent into the abyss and his projected return. Again, Herr, recalling the impact his fellow war correspondents made on him, describes Sean Flynn, photo-journalist and son of Errol, as looking as if he was 'coming out of some heavy heart-of-darkness trip' (Herr 1978: 15). The implicit structure, then, is that of the journey into chaos, the initiation into absurdity. Reminiscent of Conrad's novella, *Dispatches* is much more explicitly mythic.

Noting that Vietnam is the meeting place, at first sight arbitrary, of various, seemingly random and fragmentary narratives, Herr surmises that 'somehow, all the mythic tracks intersected' (Herr 1978: 24). The ultimate challenge, then, is to decide whether there is one essential story underlying all the rest. The abortive tale of the GI is exceptional, in that it is at least directly told. Mainly the sources are the media, and in particular the cinema. The implication is that, even as Herr seems to be experiencing the war immediately, it will assume the shape of a favoured paradigm. Hence he frequently ponders on the significance of the Western film genre – a modern, democratic variation on hero myth. John Ford's *Fort Apache*, the first in that director's cavalry trilogy, has Henry Fonda as Colonel Thursday, the new commander. A strict disciplinarian, he shows as little respect for his own men as for the neighbouring Indians. Captain York, 'the old hand' played by John Wayne, knows and respects both the soldiers and the native Americans, and tries to advise the colonel to alter his belligerent attitude. But Thursday will have none of it, and eventually leads his forces into a massacre. Significantly, Herr refers pointedly to the climax of the film, in which 'he and his command get wiped out', as a great 'mythopathic moment'. Vietnam would seem inevitably to suggest a narrative paradigm, no matter how inconclusively and absurdly.

If 'all the mythic tracks intersected', then there is always the possibility of one underlying structure. *Dispatches* does not confirm that it exists, only suggests that it might. John Hellmann has no doubts: 'Herr's narrative form – seemingly a chaotic assemblage of episodes and vignettes – actually represents a "howling" mental wilderness through which a heroic narrator journeys towards the grail of self-knowledge.' Not only that, but the 'grail' is ultimately to be found, and the tracks only intersect, in the larger terrain of American culture itself: 'The excitement of *Dispatches* for the post-Vietnam American is that it suggests Vietnam may yet be transformed into a frontier landscape affording a meaningful errand for the culture, an errand of self-examination' (Hellmann 1986: 159–60). Taking Hellmann's point, and acknowledging Herr's elision of history (Vietnam) and myth (the Western), we may yet demur at having *Dispatches* recuperated for tradition by being thus neatly incorporated into what is sometimes called the American pioneer myth, of which Vietnam would form yet another episode. Here we would go no further than to affirm that Herr's work, as a postmodernist hero myth, demonstrates the potential of the 'heart-of-darkness trip', that of intuiting cosmos in the extremes of chaos, without ever finding it. Or, to put this another way, if *The Waste Land* was informed by a 'rage for order', in *Dispatches* we have 'rage' and we have 'order' but we have no guaranteed connection between them.

3

ENDS

THE CIRCUITOUS QUEST

We have found Eliade's creation paradigm to be useful in comparing and contrasting the poetry of Eliot and that of Morrison. The key is Altizer's phrase, 'the dialectic of the sacred and the profane', which he sees as making explicit what is implicit in Eliade's mythography. However, we should bear in mind that Eliade, despite allowing for a vision of the 'coincidence of opposites', in which the sacred and the profane might be realised as aspects of each other, does not explore in any detail the historicity of this process. While he concedes that profane time is the only time in which sacred time becomes meaningful, since without the former there would be no point in projecting the latter, he pays little attention to the process of profane time itself. That is, he is content to identify the sacred with the past, with the moment of origin, and myth with that 'eternal return' by which history recovers the dimension of cosmos. In this chapter, we need to consider the mythic potential of profane time more carefully.

What we have said about the creation paradigm could be applied also to the fertility paradigm. The vegetation cycle is not the most historically promising of models for myth. Of course, we have had to distinguish between the 'tragic' interpretation of the paradigm, evident in *The Waste Land* and '*Ulysses,* Order and Myth', and the 'comic', evident in 'The Happy New Year' and 'The Returning Hero'. But both Eliot and Rickword came to a point in their careers where the initial model came to seem inadequate. Both sought to go beyond the cycle. Eliot adopted the Christian myth of deliverance and Rickword adopted the Marxist variation upon it. Both opted for a narrative which emphasised the future rather than the past.

We will consider Rickword's development first. In or around 1930 he became a member of the Communist Party, and went on to found another journal, *Left Review* (1934–8). It is worth comparing the passion of his editorial of April 1937, 'The Cultural Meaning of May Day', with the playfulness of 'The Returning Hero'. But if we are expecting a complete break with the cyclical model we will be surprised:

> What is the deepest concept in all art, the form on which all our dramas and lyrics depend? It is the concept of struggle forged by men at work, by men and women joined in harmony in the struggle against Nature. It is the story of the death and the re-birth of the Year. That was the basic theme of all the mythologies of human life. For the Year was not something apart from man, it was the living shape of the earth which man had to contend with and master.
>
> Man the Worker symbolised his productive struggle in the changes of Nature. His enemy was the Old Year, the Greybeard of hate, all that became socially resistant to advance. And he, the undaunted, was the New Year, the youth of strong thews, who fought the Old Man for the bride of spring and the childing earth of his toil. And yet both death and life were in him. He,

individually, must die, though the struggle went on. And so arose our tragedy, blessing life.

But, when the bright season came, after the fight against the plots and menaces of winter, the bride was won, the field of work was cleared; and so our comedy arose, blessing life.

Out of Man Working came all these concepts. . . .

So now we gather again on May Day, in a world where force and greed have stolen the earth away from the happy feet. This is the right day for our gathering, chosen by an insight that went to the heart of things.

(Rickword 1937: 130–1)

Curiously, Rickword's case for communism gains its resonance from Frazer's 'myth and ritual' researches; he is, after all, talking about a workers' holiday which has its roots in the Celtic spring feast of Beltain. Thus the cyclical model of 'The Returning Hero' has survived his political conversion. But now 'comedy' denotes a structural principle only, which is held quite distinct from the earlier 'comic' mood. The author of this earnest manifesto is no longer refusing to 'grow serious all at once' or 'put up with another new creed'. As with Eliot, we may trace a move through narrative to commitment. Eliot will be seen to move from *mythos* to *Logos*, to explicit faith in a distinctively Christian Word. Rickword is here seen to have rewritten *mythos* as *logos*, as the doctrine of Marxism. We may still call his position mythic, but we must recognise that the myth has been severely adapted in the service of a new kind of thinking. The crucial factor is the choice of the symbolic figure of 'Man the Worker'.

Interestingly, since there is no evidence that Rickword was acquainted with his work, Kenneth Burke put his mind to the same sort of phrasing in his address to the predominantly Communist body, the American Writers' Congress, two years before Rickword's editorial. Himself a fellow traveller rather than a party activist, he wrote his speech, 'Revolutionary Symbolism in America', to prevent Marxism becoming too arid. There are two important arguments in the address that are relevant to our discussion. Firstly, Marxism cannot ignore its mythic dimension:

> 'Myths' may be wrong, or they may be used to bad ends – but they cannot be dispensed with. In the last analysis, they are our basic psychological tools for working together. A hammer is a carpenter's tool; a wrench is a mechanic's tool; and a 'myth' is a social tool for welding the sense of inter-relationship by which the carpenter and the mechanic, though differently occupied, can work together for common social ends. In this sense a myth that works well is as real as food, tools, and shelter are.
>
> (Simons and Melia 1989: 267)

So far Rickword and Burke might be in agreement. But the second argument is this:

> The symbol I should plead for, as more basic, more of an ideal incentive, than that of the worker, is that of 'the people'. . . . The symbol of 'the people', as distinct from the proletarian symbol, also has the tactical advantage of pointing more definitely in the direction of unity (which in itself is a sound psychological tendency, for all that it is now misused by nationalists to mask the conditions of disunity). It contains the *ideal*, the ultimate *classless* feature which the revolution would bring about – and for this reason seems richer as a symbol of allegiance.
>
> (Simons and Melia 1989: 267, 270)

Burke, that is, is suggesting how to keep Marxism alive as a myth, as a symbolic story that offers hope to as many people as possible. Rickword, possibly under pressure from Stalinists in the Communist Party of Great Britain, besotted by the Five-Year Plan, feels obliged to narrow the symbolism to 'Man the Worker'. Hence

'The Cultural Meaning of May Day' is not as inclusive an exercise in mythopoeia as it might be.

Another problem with Rickword's editorial is that the Marxist vision is more usually seen as following another trajectory altogether. Like Christianity, the pattern traced by Marx's myth is meant to be essentially progressive. It treats history as an advance, proceeding stage by stage to the goal of a classless society. Where the Christian story begins with Eden and ends with Jerusalem, the Marxist begins with the primitive communism of tribal society and ends with the advanced communism of postcapitalist society. In between, in both cases, comes a series of conflicts and crises without which the historical goal cannot be reached. Adapting a useful diagram constructed by Trevor Blackwell and Jeremy Seabrook, we can outline the full story as follows:

1 Eden/primitive communism
2 the fall/the development of private property
3 the wilderness/class society
4 the crucifixion/the oppression of the proletariat
5 the resurrection/the rise of class consciousness
6 the day of judgement/the revolution
7 Jerusalem/classless society

(Blackwell and Seabrook 1988: 111)

Looked at this way, both Christianity and Marxism are myths of deliverance: both are progressive, both involve crucial choice and commitment, and both promise absolute redemption. They are 'comic' in the sense that they are oriented towards a new life ahead of us in time.

The rhetoric of 'The Cultural Meaning of May Day', then, succeeds only in so far as it forgets the orthodox interpretation of Marxism. While 'the story of the death and rebirth of the year' is a suitable context for making 'Man the Worker' our new mythic hero, *pace* Burke, it might be objected that it cannot do complete justice to that final battle in which the proletariat gains mastery of the means of production. The cyclical model would not be ultimately appropriate. And yet Rickword's prose has its power, without our having to suspend our disbelief. Marx and Frazer are an unlikely alliance, but their simultaneous use does support the main aim of the *Left Review* editor at a time of severe oppression: to express his trust in the victory of the proletariat by appeal to natural justice, or seasonal legitimacy. The spirit of revolution is evoked, even if the letter of orthodox Marxism has been revised. The 'event' of May Day, originally a fertility festival, is 'perfected', to use Burke's term, by being placed within a suitably mythic frame.

After all, as with the Christian quest, there is something unsatisfactory about the starkly progressive pattern, with its implication that the earth and its rhythms are somehow to be superseded in a perfect state. Indeed, M.H. Abrams has referred us to Marx's own definition, in *The Economic and Philosophical Manuscripts*, of the true, final 'society' as 'the veritable resurrection of nature, the realized naturalism of man and the realized humanism of nature'. What is being proposed, Abrams decides, is the model of 'the circuitous quest'. For the conception is of the end as 'a "return" to the beginning, but at a higher level'. Thus 'each man' will not only be 'rejoined with other men' but also 'reunited to a nature which is no longer dead and alien but has been resurrected and has assumed a companionable, because a human form' (Abrams 1971: 315–16). Marxism, or at least the doctrine of the early Marx, is then best identified with the historical project of Romanticism. Poets such as Wordsworth and Coleridge, Blake and Shelley, seeing themselves as 'poet–prophets', in various ways announced 'the certainty, or at least the possibility, of a rebirth in which mankind will inhabit a renovated earth where he will find himself thoroughly at home' (Abrams 1971: 12). Given what we have already noted, we might even agree with Abrams that this Romantic-Marxist ideal is a secular variant on the Christian myth, itself a 'circuitous quest'. The paradigm of deliverance is informed by the paradigm of fertility ('rebirth'), which is in turn informed by the paradigm of creation ('renovated earth'), and that informing is mutual. Jerusalem is Eden both regained and transformed.

Perhaps, then, Rickword's account of the victory of 'Man the Worker', a victory at once recurrent and progressive, is not really the distortion of Marx which orthodoxy might suggest. However, if we admit Burke's contention that Marxism is primarily a myth, then Rickword's failure is the narrowing of focus and the exclusion of possibilities entailed in his choice of symbol.

If Rickword was constrained by orthodoxy, Eliot embraced it. As we may infer from our previous discussion of *The Waste Land*, his move to Christianity was not the dramatic break with his earlier mythic interests it might otherwise seem. It is likely that Frazer suspected he had undermined Christianity by demonstrating its roots in primitive fertility worship. But Eliot went on to conclude, perhaps with Weston's help, that Jesus' affinities with Osiris and Adonis only gave him 'roots', those absent from the 'stony rubbish' of the modern wilderness. 'He who was living is now dead': that this might refer either to the god or to the son of God was an ambiguity which increased the power of Eliot's poem, and which anticipated the poet's own spiritual transition. Moreover, in so far as Jesus recalled Attis, he might be situated in terms of mystery religion, itself based on fertility religion; but that only enhanced his appeal, and did not reduce his spiritual credibility.

Eliot's transition was not inevitable, however: it is one thing to note affinities between nature/mystery cults and Christianity, in the spirit of the comparative method, and it is another to embrace the latter without reservation. The Eliot who declared himself 'classicist', 'royalist' and 'anglo-catholic' had – officially, as it were – abandoned the fertility and mystery paradigms for that of deliverance. Only, he interpreted it in such a way as to defuse its radical potential. Throughout the 1930s he was constantly trying to draw inferences from his faith about the nature and needs of his age, but felt obliged to adopt a negative stance. In *After Strange Gods*, a repudiation of what he saw as the 'heretical' interests of various literary contemporaries (Thomas Hardy and D.H. Lawrence, for example), he felt further obliged to describe his own ideal of an integrated Christian society in the face of encroaching chaos:

> The population should be homogeneous . . . . What is still more important is unity of religious background; and reasons of race and religion combine to make any large numbers of free-thinking Jews undesirable. There must be a proper balance between urban and rural, industrial and agricultural development. And a spirit of excessive tolerance is to be deprecated.
>
> (Eliot 1934: 19–20)

We cannot help but recall Burke's reminder of the dangers of the logic of 'perfectionism': extreme adherence to an 'ideal order' is totalitarian. If we test Eliot's vision against the grand narrative of redemption outlined above, we can see that his is not progressive but deeply conservative: indeed, wholly reactionary. Rather than anticipating the liberation of all humanity from the bonds of sin, he looks backwards to an order that is not only hierarchical but also exclusive. In other words, he is more interested in defending Christendom and past perfection (as he perceives it) than in promoting Christianity and future possibility. The myth of deliverance has been distorted into a dogma of denial and, to adopt *The Calendar*'s usage, 'repression'. Nor can the model of 'the circuitous quest' be relied on here: in the salvational perspective, Jerusalem might be Eden regained and transformed, but it certainly cannot be medieval Europe revisited.

Thus we can see Rickword and Eliot as engaged in two different attempts to relate myth and history. The one runs the risk of distorting the progressive ideal by privileging the circular over the progressive metaphor. But he achieves his rhetorical effect, despite being at odds with the early, Romantic Marx, to the extent that he figures social transformation in exclusive not inclusive terms. The other is consistently imbalanced: the Christian narrative is distorted from the start by the fantasy of a harmonious Christendom, by the retreat from history into the myth of cultural purity. Worse still, this involves the complete repudiation of not only 'excessive tolerance' but also the rights of a whole people. Written the year after Hitler became the German Chancellor, with his declared anti-semitic programme, *After Strange Gods* shows how completely a myth may overpower, rather than simply 'order', one's sense of history.

THE RHETORIC OF REVELATION

It is now necessary to consider the myth of deliverance at more leisure. There are two reasons for this, one general and one specific. Firstly, we should be aware of how the narrative which still informs Western culture and literature came to be articulated, as itself a cultural and literary expression. Myth does not arise from nowhere, and in the case of the Biblical myth we can watch the myth-making at work. Secondly, if the Book of Exodus is the earliest version of the myth of deliverance, the one that is much more explicitly and consciously mythical is the Book of Revelation. In studying its apocalyptic myth, we can provide a context for subsequent visions of the end – notably, of course, *Apocalypse Now.*

The myth of deliverance is oriented forwards: though it assumes a hierarchy, in the form of a heaven above, it also assumes a horizon, in the form of a promised land or Messianic kingdom. Implying a movement of time towards a decisive culmination, this kind of myth is called 'eschatological' (Greek *eskhatos*, 'last'). Instead of the annual recurrence of the seasonal cycle, and instead of the cosmic order, we think of the last days of history.

Eschatological myths which envisage an abrupt, usually violent break between the present order and a new existence, and a total transformation of the world, are called 'apocalyptic'. The word 'apocalypse' is a transliteration of the Greek word for revelation: hence such myths uncover the mystery or hidden meaning of the end. Historical existence as previously understood will, we learn, be over; and then we will know a state in which eternity and history, sacred time and profane time, are fused. The ending is decisive: at once a closure to one kind of life and a transition to another, 'unprecedented' mode of existence. Out of catastrophe comes a new cosmos. The Judaeo-Christian Bible culminates in a major apocalyptic work, the Book of Revelation.

Incongruous as it may sound, Jim Morrison, in the song which features on the soundtrack of *Apocalypse Now*, is working within the Biblical tradition, as must anyone who announces an absolute ending. Though Coppola uses the lyric to accompany the sequence in which Willard kills Kurtz, and in so doing evokes the fertility paradigm, it certainly suits the title of his film. 'This is the end,' it declares: the end of 'all our elaborate plans'; the end of 'ev'rything that stands' (Doors 1992: 18–19). Coppola's film itself draws its power, however indirectly, from Revelation. The Vietnam war was a catastrophe that merits the epithet 'apocalyptic'; and the epithet has its scriptural connotations. However, there is an attendant question which we have to ask: what can it mean to speak of *Apocalypse* as *Now*? The film may be mythic in its scale, stretching from the sacred grove of Nemi to the napalm-scarred landscape of Vietnam, but how can it actually be about the last days? The short answer is that it cannot, but that it need not be. In what follows we may come to accept that that is an enigma intrinsic to the apocalyptic genre itself. We will first consider the Book of Revelation; and then, by way of another glimpse at *The Waste Land*, we will reconsider *Apocalypse Now* in the light of Revelation.

The Book of Revelation was written in about 90 AD. Nero had ruled the Roman empire in 54–68 AD, and had been succeeded by Domitian. Both were savage persecutors of the followers of Jesus of Nazareth, who had been executed by the Romans earlier in the century. These Jewish followers, whose ranks were being swelled by Gentiles, were derisively known as 'Christians', because they believed their leader to have been 'the Christ', the anointed one, the Messiah. In order to test their loyalty to the empire, Christians were required to worship the emperor himself as a god and Rome itself as a goddess ('Roma'). John the Divine, as he came to be known (to distinguish him from John the Evangelist), wrote Revelation in order to encourage the persecuted communities of Christians – in particular, the seven churches of Asia Minor. He claimed to have had a vision on the island of Patmos (off the coast of present-day Turkey): this would, he hoped, inspire the faithful to withstand persecution. Above all, they were to hold fast to the promise of Christ's second coming, when he was expected to return again to earth, after his crucifixion, resurrection and ascension to heaven, in order to judge the living and the dead.

In brief, the story Revelation tells is that of the Messiah, figured simultaneously as 'Lamb' and as 'Lion of the tribe of Judah', defeating the dragon who is Satan, and establishing his thousand-year reign or millennium. Key figures and moments in this drama of salvation are as follows. There are the four horsemen of the apocalypse: conquest, blood, famine and death. There is the woman clothed with the sun, giving birth to a son, probably the Messiah, whom the archangel Michael has to rescue from the clutches of the dragon. There is the beast whose number is 'Six hundred threescore and six', in later Christian tradition to be known as the 'Antichrist'; the people are forced to wear his mark; probably, if the logic of numerology is applied to the Greek alphabet, his name spells out 'Emperor Nero'. There is the 'whore of Babylon', who lives in luxury by oppressing the mass of the people; she is probably Rome itself, the author using the code name of a previous oppressor of God's people. There is the subjugation of Satan by Jesus in his capacity as Messianic warrior, appearing on a white horse; 'and he that sat upon him was called Faithful and True, and in righteousness he doth judge and make war' (Revelation 19: 11). There is the penultimate moment of the battle between the forces of good and evil at Armageddon. And then there is the final vision of 'a new heaven and a new earth', ruled from a holy city called Jerusalem; there will be no more tears and no more death; in the middle of the city will be a tree – the tree of life which Adam and Eve were denied after the fall.

Eliade would read this narrative as circular in implication. That is, sacred time is recovered, and we experience a moment of regeneration, by which cosmos re-emerges out of chaos; only, it is placed at the end of profane time and not at the beginning. But we have already indicated that the myth of deliverance does not depict Jerusalem as a simple repetition of Eden, the primordial paradise. Though the tree of life is restored, it is now placed in a celestial city ruled by the son of God. According to the 'circuitous quest' paradigm, the end is the beginning transformed, on a higher level; it takes on a whole new significance because it is informed by the long struggle through the wilderness of sin and death, during which God's people endure a sequence of oppression (bondage in Egypt, exile in Babylon, persecution by Rome).

However we envisage the implicit structure of the grand narrative which the Bible as a whole recounts, the point to remember is that the recounting always takes place in a specific book (Exodus, Isaiah, Daniel, Revelation), and that book is primarily a response to its own day. John the Divine addresses his contemporaries; he may be talking about the future, but his primary concern is how he and they may endure persecution in the here and now. Indeed, the very promise of Christ's second coming is always a present promise. What matters chiefly is the act of waiting for the end. As we read in the Gospels: 'when ye shall hear of wars and rumours of wars, be ye not troubled: for such things must needs be; but the end shall not be yet' (Mark 13: 7). The readers of Revelation exist in a moment of eschatological tension: they believe that Jesus has indeed saved them, has fulfilled the promise of the exodus, by virtue of his resurrection; but meanwhile they must await the signs of the final victory over Satan. They exist between the 'already' and the 'not yet'. Both past promise and future possibility exist in the here and now.

The Book of Revelation, then, is an intervention in history rather than a transcendent overview of the meaning of history, but its claim to visionary status is essential to its appeal and its effect. However, while the proclamation that the end is nigh is a useful tactic for inspiring and consolidating the faithful, it must be recognised to be primarily a matter of language (it is written in the form of a letter to the church communities) and of projection (it is a letter written at a particular moment of crisis). The issue of whether the text is revealed truth must remain an open question. What we can say is that Revelation is a magnificent work of visionary rhetoric. It is an extraordinary example of what Kenneth Burke calls 'symbolic action': a textual 'strategy' designed to meet a given 'situation'. Without the latter, the intense historical constraint, there would be no need to try and extend language to the limit. But given that ambition, the symbolic act becomes also 'the dancing of an attitude', an imaginative exploration (Burke 1989: 77–85). From the particular moment of persecution, then, Revelation takes the promise of deliverance, and pushes it 'to the end of the line', as Burke would have it. Once its author has recognised the dilemma – that Christians suffer and that Rome flourishes, that the poor and the good are oppressed by the rich and the evil – then the whole saving myth may be generated, so to speak. In so far as there is a conflict, there must also be a narrative. There must be a Christ and an Antichrist, a bride and a whore, a warrior on a white horse and a dragon with two attendant beasts; and so there must be a final and absolutely decisive battle.

Moreover, because the focus of the rhetoric must be the audience, we have to ask ourselves how Revelation works on its reader, how it fulfils its strategic function. Elizabeth Fiorenza considers John's text in the light of Burke's thinking about the relation between verbal arrangement and vital effect. She agrees with him that the 'mythic' structure is also a 'ritual' structure: not in Frazer's sense, but rather because it 'follows the form of a cathartic journey'. This crucial inner voyage 'moves the audience from alienation through purification to redemption'. Experiencing an emotional 'separating out', it sees its own 'passion (persecution and suffering) . . . transformed into an assertion'. That is: 'In taking his audience on the dramatic-cathartic journey of Rev., John seeks to "move" them to control their fear and to sustain their vision' (Fiorenza 1985: 198).

This is not, then, 'myth and ritual' according to either Frazer's fertility or Eliade's creation paradigm. It is not that a whole society is focusing attention on a god who dies and revives. Nor, although there is a cosmic battle between divine warrior and dragon, are we to think in terms of eternal return. Rather, an oppressed minority is purging itself of fear by attending to a language that creatively turns the world upside down, transforming defeat into victory. Here myth, as rhetoric, becomes a verbal ritual. It effects an identification – of the individual with her faith, and of the individual with her fellow Christians. This it does by persuading her of a transformation: that is, the historical time of suffering (*chronos*) becomes the crucial time in which a new cosmos comes out of catastrophe (*kairos*).

If we can accept that Revelation is rhetorical, and that apocalypse is always effectively now, we will not be surprised to find secular writers putting John's paradigm to their own contemporary use. In the first book of Edmund Spenser's *The Fairie Queene* (1590), the Red Cross Knight is commissioned by Gloriana, Queen of Fairy Land, to accompany a young woman called Una to the kingdom of her parents and deliver them from a dragon that is laying waste their land. This poem, written in honour of Elizabeth I, is what we might call a Tudor apocalypse: its rhetorical purpose is to celebrate her reign as a variation upon the model of the millennium. It is no coincidence that in the first canto, we read of the knight, 'Right faithfull true he was in deede and word'; and of the lady, that 'by her in line a milke white lambe she had' (Spenser 1966: 4). The echoes from Revelation are deliberate: the knight's quest is meant to remind us of Christ's apocalyptic battle; and so Una's parents may be identified with Adam and Eve, their land with Eden and the dragon with Satan. But more is intended even than this. 'Una' signifies the one true Protestant faith of England. The dragon signifies all the various threats to the Reformation. The specific threat of Catholic idolatory is represented by Duessa, the witch of falsehood, who tries to lead the knight astray, and who is reminiscent of the 'whore of Babylon'. And so the knight's quest is also that of ensuring that Gloriana's (Queen Elizabeth's) land remains true to the spirit of her Tudor predecessor Henry VIII. Her court in London can then approximate to Jerusalem, the heavenly city. And appropriately enough, no sooner is his quest completed and the battle against the dragon won, than the Red Cross Knight is revealed to be none other than St George, patron saint of England. Strictly speaking, then, *The Fairie Queene* may be characterised as a reactionary use of Revelation's rhetoric, in that its aim is to confirm the established hierarchy, not to offer a horizon of hope to the oppressed. The authoritarianism of Christendom thus replaces the revolutionary impetus of primitive Christianity.

This becomes obvious when we contrast Spenser's poem with the political prose of Gerrard Winstanley, the leader of 'the Diggers or True Levellers' during the English Revolution of the seventeenth century. For him, it was not only Anglicanism and monarchy which embodied the status quo, but also Cromwell and the leaders of the republic – none of whom represented the interests of the poor artisans or the peasants. They still adhered to a world of power and property because they had not acknowledged the radical and apocalyptic spirit of Christ. Thus *Fire in the Bush* (1650) alludes on its title page to 'The great Battle of God Almighty, between Michael the Seed of Life, and the great red Dragon, the curse, fought within the Spirit of Man'. Winstanley identifies 'the power of darkness' with the 'dragon' in the human soul, 'which causes all wars and sorrows' and is 'the son of bondage, which must not abide in the heart for ever but must be cast out'. For 'Christ the annointing spirit doth not enslave any, but comes to set all free', to pull off 'all mourning weeds' and to 'wipe away all tears' (Winstanley 1973: 211–17). That last phrase, a direct quotation from Revelation, is taken as a political programme as well as a religious promise. Winstanley's Christ guarantees an end to the unnecessary suffering which results from an unjust society.

Both *The Fairie Queene* and *Fire in the Bush*, then, are variations on the myth of deliverance, as dramatised by the Book of Revelation. The former emphasises the already; the latter emphasises the not yet. But both are responses to the present: the former wants to justify it; the latter wants to repudiate it. The former assumes the given hierarchy to be divinely ordained; the latter wishes to topple it in the name of Christ. Both are 'symbolic acts', but the former works hard to equate the symbolism of apocalypse with stasis, while the latter takes from John the Divine's text the understanding that all symbols are promises, figures of possibility. The rhetoric of Revelation is rich enough to sustain both alternatives, and perhaps many others. For example, in the modern age we find D.H. Lawrence, whose own work culminates in a study of John the Divine's text, propounding an eschatology of sexual resurrection. *Lady Chatterley's Lover* (1928), in which the female hero is initiated into the mysteries of carnal love (including anal sex) by her gamekeeper, is an ostensibly realistic novel which may be easily translated into visionary terms: 'Mellors, in the England of Lloyd George, is the Saint George who kills the dragon (the serpent of corruption, of shame at defecation) and sets the

lady free; an act as apocalyptic as that of Spenser's St George'
(Kermode 1973: 131). Deliverance and fertility here are made to
coincide; the not yet of a nation's transformation is shown to be
realised in the already of the sexual act. Needless to say, Spenser
would not have approved, despite the above analogy; nor, for that
matter, would Winstanley.

APOCALYPSE WITHOUT APOCALYPSE

Study of the Book of Revelation reminds us forcibly of the way
myth may work on history, and vice versa. However, as we have
already seen, the modernism of Eliot is based on the premiss that
myth and history are opposed, the one offering transcendence
of the other. Here we want to consider *Apocalypse Now*, a postmodernist film, as a work in which the intimate relation between
myth and history becomes of interest once more. The 'apocalypse'
of its title has something to do with this, of course, and so perhaps
we need to situate the film in relation to both Eliot and John the
Divine.

Frank Kermode has suggested that *The Waste Land* might be
related to Revelation in so far as it depicts a demonic metropolis,
ripe for destruction. He quotes from John the Divine's account of
the fall of Babylon, that city personified by a 'whore': 'And the
merchants of the earth shall weep and mourn over her . . . saying,
Alas, the great city, that was clothed in fine linen, and purple, and
scarlet, and decked with gold, and precious stones, and pearls! For
in one hour so great riches is come to naught.' He comments:
'This is the London of *The Waste Land*, the City by the sea
with its remaining flashes of inexplicable imperial splendour:
the Unreal City, the *urbs aeterna* declined into *l'immonde cité*'
(Kermode 1990: 308–9). But there is an ambiguity underlying
Eliot's use of Revelation, expressive as that book is of contempt
for all worldly empires, and in particular Rome. For the 'eternal'
city of the classical Latin poet Virgil (author of the *Aeneid*, which

celebrates the founding of Rome) remains the yardstick by which to measure the modern decadence of Baudelaire's 'unclean' or 'impure' city. Committed to the ideal civilisation of Virgil, to the true, everlasting essence of Rome underlying its manifest corruption, Eliot wishes to identify squalor and spiritual poverty only with the contemporary city. In doing so, he finds the rhetoric of Revelation congenial, but 'behind the temporal disaster of Babylon he knows that the timeless pattern of the eternal city must survive' (Kermode 1990: 309). The imagery of disaster and that of continuity coexist. Myth remains aloof from history, and Revelation is read as somehow transcending the sense of crisis and catastrophe which occasioned its desperate rhetoric.

With *Apocalypse Now* the sense of crisis and catastrophe predominates, as is appropriate in a film about Vietnam. Atrocity follows atrocity, in this postmodern war, to no apparent purpose. Thus we find Colonel Kilgore leading a bombing raid on a Vietnamese village to the sound of Wagner, in order to clear the beach area for a surfing display. Again, we find the Do Lung bridge being manned by leaderless, drug-hallucinating soldiers, shelling an invisible enemy, merely so the generals can say that the bridge is open. If out of these symptoms of chaos we infer a narrative pattern, we are hard put to name it. Kilgore's massacre and the Do Lung fiasco become eschatological signs of an ending which is immanent rather than imminent, chronically pervasive rather than critically forthcoming. This is a postmodernist film, the appropriate response to a postmodern war. Eliot's hierarchy, his identification of myth with transcendent truth, is not available. But nor is any other position, apparently. Myth here is dispersed in history.

That is, where Eliot's myth was a means of controlling 'the futility and anarchy which is contemporary history', Coppola makes no distinction between myth and history, order and chaos, Nemi and Vietnam. Ultimately, perhaps, there is not even any distinction between Eliot's poetry and Colonel Kurtz's recitation of it in the depths of his Cambodian temple. What matters is the image. Any narrative we discern in *Apocalypse Now* is built up by the juxtaposition of images: the tribespeople slaying the buffalo (primitivist motif); the bombing of the temple (apocalyptic motif); Kurtz's reading matter, lingered over by the camera (modernist motif); and so on, right back to the assignment of Willard to the mission, as in the Grail legend (romance motif) and the opening sequence in which he confronts his demonic double in the mirror (Gothic and/or psychoanalytic motif). The effect is that of cultural tourism, moving through both space and time. Though Eliot spoke of the 'presence' of the past, the effect intended was quite different. *The Waste Land* was preoccupied with 'roots'; *Apocalypse Now* is preoccupied with 'routes'. What William Carlos Williams predicted has happened: the 'pure products of culture' have gone 'crazy', and all one can do is make one's way through the bewildering array without ever expecting to find a position of final fixity (Clifford 1986: 1–17). Chaos is certain; cosmos is hypothetical.

The import of this discovery is that we must not speak of 'myth' but must speak of 'myths'. Eliot could shape a whole modernist epic poem around Frazer's dying god, as refigured in Weston's Grail monarch, confident that he had found a universal and eternal order transcending the disorder of his day. Coppola offers us imagery from the same sources but hesitates to grant it any further status. Such visual allusions are on a par with all the others in the film; and all of them may be illusions. Here are icons whose sacred significance is in question. Where Eliot worked on the assumption that beneath or beyond all his words there resided the Word, waiting to be recovered, Coppola addresses the possibility that beyond the image there need be nothing at all; beneath the signifier there need be no signified. Hence even if several scenes from *Apocalypse Now* are reminiscent of John the Divine's vision of the end, that vision has now been cast adrift from the grand narrative of deliverance which originally gave it meaning, and we are left with floating intimations of a cosmic transformation that will never happen.

Thus we reach the paradox of Coppola's vision. This turns out not to centre on the film's title since, as I have demonstrated, all *Apocalypse* is *Now*; the revelation of the end of history always takes place in history, and for good rhetorical purposes. The tension we are interested in is not that between present and future, but that between present and present. It is between the present of the already and the present of the not yet.

Perhaps we could illuminate this tension in the context of the postmodern by briefly tracing the way the French philosopher Jacques Derrida changed his mind in the space of little more than a decade. Here we will juxtapose two statements, one from 1981 (translated the following year) and the other from 1994. Writing two years after the release of *Apocalypse Now*, Derrida reflects on the fact that virtually the last main sentence of the Book of Revelation is the exhortation, 'Even so, come, lord Jesus.' He sees that one word 'come' as the clue to our postmodern apocalypse, since the more it is looked at the more it resists definition. It addresses us from that elsewhere which is always just the other side of where we are:

> Now here, precisely, is announced – as promise or threat – an apocalypse without apocalypse . . . without last judgment, without any other eschatology than the tone of the 'Come' itself, its very difference, an apocalypse beyond good and evil. 'Come' does not announce this or that apocalypse: already it resounds with a certain tone; it is in itself the apocalypse of the apocalypse; 'Come' is apocalyptic. Our *apocalypse now* . . .
>
> (Derrida 1982: 94)

The rhetoric of Revelation still fulfils a function, in that it unsettles, disturbs, 'deconstructs' the present. The narrative promise of the not yet survives the loss of doctrinal belief; the challenge of apocalypse may be felt without the religious meaning of apocalypse. Or we might say, in a reversal of Bultmann, *mythos* is what matters, not *Logos* (sacred Word) or *kerygma* (scriptural message).

Between this first statement of Derrida's and the second comes Francis Fukuyama's *The End of History and the Last Man* (1992), which proclaims 'apocalypse now' in a different sense. The Messianic kingdom is already, and it has taken the form of Western, liberal democracy. Capitalism has won; Marxism and other modes of resistance are dead. The historical project advocated by Marx is now defunct, and the symbol of the free market entrepreneur has permanently replaced that of the militant proletariat. Derrida's response is caustic. He begins by invoking Marx's declaration at the beginning of *The Communist Manifesto* (1848): 'A spectre is haunting Europe – the spectre of communism.' He insists that 'the inheritance of Marxism' is still alive, because inheritance 'is never a given, it is always a task'. Far from assuming democracy to have been established, it is necessary 'to speak of a democracy *to come*'. He now addresses the theme of global justice, neglected by Fukuyama:

> Instead of singing the advent of the ideal of liberal democracy and the capitalist market in the euphoria of the end of history, instead of celebrating the 'end of all ideologies' and the end of the great emancipatory discourses, let us never neglect this obvious macroscopic fact, made up of innumerable singular sites of suffering: no degree of progress allows one to ignore that never before, in absolute figures, never have so many men, women, and children been subjugated, starved, or exterminated on the Earth.
>
> (Derrida 1994: 53)

Given Fukuyama's apocalyptic pronouncement, which has destroyed the creative tension between the already and the not yet,

Derrida feels obliged to disassociate himself completely from the rhetoric of Revelation. It has become tainted. So, in posing again the question of justice, he endorses (without committing himself to Marxism) the fundamental concerns of Marx. That is, he invokes (despite his own hostility to 'mythology', a word synonymous for him with Western thinking and the illusions of origin, presence and Word) the myth of deliverance. He invokes it, though, not in its apocalyptic but in its historical aspect. He refuses to accept 'the end of history' if that means also the end of the struggle on behalf of the oppressed.

Coppola's apocalypse, I would suggest, must not be understood in terms of Fukuyama's scenario. It already is the now of crisis and catastrophe, not of smooth settlement. Thoroughly mythic and anti-doctrinal, it forces the viewer to inhabit a moment of endless, traumatic transition, in which Babylon is continually about to fall and Armageddon about to be fought. Justice is absent, but the viewer is forced to confront that absence. Far from setting aside the issues of power and oppression, the film articulates them through images that remain mythic even as their supporting narrative is put into question. If these 'fragments' are not 'shored' against ruin, as Eliot has it in *The Waste Land*, they demand that we sketch some structure for ourselves, fragile as it might be. Where Fukuyama cuts short the promise of apocalypse, denying the very historical anxiety which gives it its power, Coppola asks us to see the vision through to the point where it almost might end.

Here we come back, finally, to the relation between myth and paradigm. We have said before that the modernist 'rage for order' has different manifestations, ranging from Eliot's 'mythical method' to Stevens's own 'Supreme Fiction'. We have also said that with postmodernism, there is an exploratory interaction between 'rage' and 'order', chaos and cosmos, as with Morrison's neoshamanism. It would be naive to contrast modernist mythopoeia and postmodernist mythopoeia as simply synonymous with order and chaos, as if these were mutually exclusive principles. Myth, after all, is inseparable from the idea of totality; yet myth has only ever been a gesture towards it. It may posit a perfect beginning, or paradise, or it may posit a perfect ending, a Messianic kingdom, but the point is that it always does so 'in the midst', between the two (Kermode 1967: 7). Myth, then, is the exemplary form of Aristotle's 'plot': it follows the rhythm of temporal experience (chronology) and yet, by virtue of its organisation, it approximates to a timeless paradigm which can never quite be realised (eternity). Kenneth Burke thinks of myth as 'the temporalising of essence', for where it speaks of origins and 'firsts' (the first day of creation, the first man and woman, the first sacrificial offering) it is always speaking simultaneously of the nature of things as understood here and now. 'Principals' are also 'principles' (Burke 1966: 381). The same goes for 'ends', which are as 'essential' as origins. Language and humanity alike are 'rotten with perfection', which certainly has its positive aspect. For unless we were 'goaded by the spirit of hierarchy', we would not stir ourselves to make narrative sense of the world (Burke 1966: 16). Words about planting and reaping, living and dying, inevitably produce words about gods and goddesses, creation and apocalypse – eventually leading all the way up to God, the one Word. And it is here that the positive aspect meets the negative. For Burke, while suggesting that 'perfectionism' is inevitable, also suggests that, knowing this, we still have a choice as to where we start from.

We can see what he means when we apply his principle to Eliot and Coppola. Eliot starts from the point of view of perfection and hierarchy, and then works downwards: he views time from the aspect of eternity. Coppola starts from the fallen world, in its most barbaric manifestation, and proceeds from there. As motif follows motif, and allusion follows allusion, we begin to form a narrative, which in turn implies a pattern. That pattern is endlessly implicit, and will never be attained. But both the director and the audience of the film cannot help but infer it –

which amounts to improvising it. Thus, just as John the Divine produced, out of the most challenging historical circumstances, a text that is still regarded as the perfect apocalyptic myth, in which cosmos is reaffirmed out of chaos, so does Coppola produce a film that, we might say, is exactly appropriate as an apocalyptic myth for our age. It is appropriate, not because it reimposes order on disorder, as does Eliot, for we can no longer believe in that kind of victory. It is appropriate because it starts from the appropriate place, in an age that knows more about chaos than it does about cosmos, and more about imperfection than perfection. If myth is ultimately about possibility, that place will always be appropriate.

II

MYTHIC READING

INTRODUCTION TO
PART II

In some measure, people already accept that language creates reality. They know that writers create. They know that saying 'Done' may create a contract, and saying 'I thee wed' may create a marriage . . . . They know that to increase your knowledge and your power in any field, you must increase your vocabulary. Articulacy is power. Your vocabulary shapes your world for you and enables you to get a grip on it. Conversely, the limits of your language are the limits of your world. All this, people know already. We add a further consideration: the end of the philosophers' dream, that the human mind could altogether outsoar the limits of language and history and lay hold of absolute speculative knowledge, is a great event. In religious thought it means giving up the attempt to transcend our myths and symbols, and returning into language.

(Cupitt 1990: ix)

What Don Cupitt declares as theologian, to his fellow Christians, may also be proposed in the present context. His declaration is particularly appropriate, since what we have been discovering in Part I is the primacy of myth – and so of language, narrative and history – over abstract ideas of eternal truth. Profane time produces sacred time, and not vice versa.

In Part II we will be spelling out the consequences of this discovery. Though Eliot, Coppola and Morrison will from now only be passing references, we should find that inferences made from their work begin to acquire some coherence. What we will be doing is taking an overview of the history of mythography, roughly from Plato to the present. But we will simultaneously be indicating the development of literary mythopoeia, roughly from Homer to the present. And as we proceed, it should become apparent that reading myth (mythography) and making myth (mythopoeia) are complementary activities. Indeed, they both involve mythic reading.

Chapter 4 will establish our two main kinds of mythic reading: allegory, which we will be identifying as 'realist'; and typology, which we will be identifying, at least in its radical form, as 'nonrealist'. Homer and Plato will be our reference points for the former; Joachim of Fiore and Dante for the latter. The two kinds of reading will be further illustrated, respectively, by such Enlightenment mythographers as C.G. Heyne and by the Romantic poet William Blake. Chapter 5 will return us to the twentieth century. Sigmund Freud, despite his debt to the Enlightenment and despite the limits of his contribution to literary criticism, will be regarded as a radical typologist, as will the novelist Franz Kafka. Carl Jung, Freud's disciple and rival, will be regarded as an allegorist; so too will the structuralist anthropologist Claude Lévi-Strauss. Finally, in Chapter 6, we will find the cultural critic Roland Barthes to equivocate between the two kinds of reading, as does the Marxist literary critic, Fredric Jameson. Interestingly, despite his reputation as a Jungian, essentialist thinker, the 'archetypal' literary critic Northrop Frye will turn out to be radically typological; and the cultural historian Marina Warner and the novelist Margaret Atwood will add further evidence of the potential of this kind of mythic reading.

4

TRUTH

REALISM AND NON-REALISM

From the quotation with which we have begun Part II, we can see that Cupitt is asking his readers to acknowledge what we have already heard Burke say, that the idea of perfection is generated by the nature of language. Or, as Burke also insists: 'the Word' is begotten by 'words'; religion is primarily a kind of rhetoric (Burke 1970: 7). For both thinkers, the theologian and the literary critic, this urge to completion leads ultimately to hierarchy. Nor are they at variance on the need to view sceptically the spatial models, whether cosmic or social, that we seem to want to create. While Burke sees 'perfectionism' as necessary, or at least inevitable, he commends learning to stand back from our own received hierarchy with the 'irony' implicit in the phrase 'rotten with perfection' (Burke 1966: 18–22). Cupitt may seem to go further, but in effect he is endorsing this need to resist attributing independent validity to our own invented systems. He makes explicit what in Burke we have so far taken to be implicit, that language and myth can never be final. *Logos* is the effect of *mythos*, and not vice versa; though words they may imply an eternal Word, they are always temporal. Because we and our world are constituted in language, we are always in process, in history. The best thing we can do is forgo the dream of a wordless world beyond this world, and take pleasure in the endless self-generating power of myth.

Thus for Cupitt, as for Burke, the ideas of hierarchy and perfection are to be treated sceptically. But what of that third dimension which we have called, following Ricoeur, possibility? We have already seen that, though the myth of deliverance suggests a final end of history, an eschatological moment of completion, apocalypse cannot help but be a present projection, a response to historical crisis. The already and the not yet both exist in the here and now. The myth of the future (deliverance), like that of the past (creation), is always about the present. Thus Ricoeur, while insisting on 'the principle of hope', denies the notion of a future totality. The point about his 'possible worlds' is that they are always 'possible'. One of the main reasons we need 'the *eschatological* sense' of some final 'unity of truth' is in order to counter the received wisdom of our own times; the story and symbolism of the 'Last Day' offer a necessary refusal of a life that has become oppressive (Ricoeur 1965: 190–1).

Myth, then, for Ricoeur is synonymous with a 'social imagination' which functions by virtue of a dialectic between 'ideology' and 'utopia'. The former, which is a necessary condition of 'integration', need not become oppressive so long as the latter is kept alive. 'On the one hand, imagination may function to preserve an order . . . . On the other hand, though, imagination may have a disruptive function; it may work as a breakthrough.' Ideology represents the first kind of imagination: 'it has the function of preservation, of conservation'. Utopia represents the second kind of imagination: 'it is always the glance from nowhere' (Ricoeur 1986: 266). Without the first kind, we would have no sense of society or tradition; without the second kind, we would simply equate the given society and tradition with eternal truth, never challenging or reforming them. Utopia prevents ideology becoming a claustrophobic system; ideology prevents utopia becoming an empty fantasy. Myth, or the social imagination, involves both. As such, it necessitates a temporal engagement, not a gesture of transcendence. Commenting on the sociologist Karl Mannheim's 'paradox' that we are always caught between the two poles, Ricoeur expresses his own dialectical conviction:

> There is no answer . . . except to say that we must try to cure the illness of utopia by what is wholesome in ideology – by its element of identity, which is once more a fundamental function of life – and try to cure the rigidity, the petrification, of ideologies by the utopian element . . . . My more ultimate answer is that we must let ourselves be drawn into the circle and then must try to make the circle a spiral. We cannot eliminate from a social ethics the element of risk. We wager on a certain set of values and then try to be consistent with them; verification is therefore a question of our whole life. No one can escape this.
>
> (Ricoeur 1986: 312)

Thus the present exists as a tension between the way things have always been and the way things ought to be. Myth, for Ricoeur, is all about this dialectic of past and future; it is a narrative whose beginning and ending continually inform the middle. Similarly, Cupitt tells us that the prophet always has to speak or be understood in terms of origins and futures (for example, 'the restoration of the primal time of perfection'), even though his business is the here and now. Alternatively, 'he may do deliberate violence to meanings by way of trying to forge a new language to describe the new reality, or, more subtly, he may seek surreptitiously to feed in new meanings by the use of irony' (Cupitt 1982: 131).

Burke too relates myth to 'irony', which he takes to be synonymous with 'dialectic' (Burke 1989: 247). The present order should always be subject to 'perspective by incongruity'. Instead of taking the current model of perfection for granted, we should always produce a 'comic corrective':

> The Church thought of man as a prospective citizen of heaven. In time, the critical inaccuracy that such transcendental emphasis brought to the gauging of material relationships became bureaucratically exploited to its limits. Out of this overemphasis, a purely antithetical overemphasis developed. Against man as a citizen of heaven, thinkers opposed man in nature; and with the progress of efficiency in reasoning, we got simply to *man in the jungle*. A comic synthesis of these antithetical emphases would 'transcend' them by stressing *man in society*.
>
> (Burke 1989: 263)

The word 'transcend' here is of course itself ironic, since Burke's whole point is that heaven, nature and society are always subject to further imaginative exploration – as, indeed, is 'man'. In short, the 'comic frame' considers human life as a project 'in composition', and where church leaders and philosophers may think they are uttering the truth, they are really only composing and recomposing the story of humanity (Burke 1989: 264, 266).

Thus Burke, Ricoeur and Cupitt agree that to recognise the primacy of language is to recognise that we are always involved in history. Moreover, it is through language and it is in history that we make our myths. In doing so, we suppress neither the past nor the future, but remain open to the potential of both. The only error is to posit an independent and self-validating truth beyond the temporal process of myth-making.

At stake here are two philosophies which Cupitt calls 'realism' and 'non-realism'. The word 'realism' is, of course, frequently used in literary criticism, especially in studying the nineteenth-century novel. This usage does relate to the philosophical definition, but we are here thinking mainly of the latter. In the philosophical sense, then, 'realism' is the belief that there exists a reality beyond or beneath the universe we articulate through language. This belief in turn may be further considered as moving through two main phases, in line with the words 'beyond' and 'beneath' in our definition. Traditional realism assumes this reality to exist 'beyond' language, in the form of some ultimate and absolute essence; this might be called the Good, or God, or the Word. Modern realism assumes this reality to exist 'beneath' language, as when Marxists take literally Marx's architectural metaphor of 'real foundations' (economic 'base' as opposed to cultural 'superstructure'). It is this sense of realism which is implicit in the discussion of fiction, referred to above: thus we often hear nineteenth-century novels being praised for their 'reflection' or 'representation' of the nineteenth-century 'world'. The main point to emphasise here is that both traditional realism and modern realism are committed to the notion of an essential truth apart from the words we use and the stories we invent to project it: the former conceives that truth to be transcendent, while the latter conceives it to be immanent. The two notions are reverse sides of the same conceptual coin (Cupitt 1986: 222).

To both versions of realism Cupitt opposes what he calls 'non-realism' (or, more dramatically, 'anti-realism'). The term would seem to have originated with Nietzsche, and it has had an important influence on twentieth-century thought. According to Cupitt the basic idea is that of 'perspectivism': 'there are many perspectival viewpoints, but there is no absolute and perspective-less vision of things' (Cupitt 1986: 223). What we call reality is effectively the result of linguistic activity: that is, before we can have a Word or a world, we need to have words. For the non-realist, then, 'we are the only makers of meanings, truths and values, and our theoretical postulates, such as God, gravity and justice, have no being apart from the language in which we speak of them and the practical uses to which we put it' (Cupitt 1995: 148). In short, realism is the illusion of truth; non-realism is the truth of illusion.

It might be useful to set out our scheme in diagrammatic form:

TRADITIONAL REALISM   NON-REALISM
Word

                                  words

world
MODERN REALISM   NON-REALISM

Put like this, we could easily situate the key figures we have discussed in Part I. Eliot, for example, would count as a traditional realist while still being a modernist poet, given that 'modernist' and 'modern' are by no means the same. Again, the Rickword of 'The Returning Hero' would count as a non-realist; but the Rickword of 'The Cultural Meaning of May Day' would be seen to be trying very hard to be a modern realist. Eliade would ultimately be a traditional realist, despite Altizer's attempts to turn him into a non-realist. Finally, Morrison, Herr and Coppola would all be non-realists. It should be stressed, however, that non-realism is not to be simply identified as postmodern: it may be traced back over the centuries to the early years of Christendom. But that is a matter to be considered more fully later.

Traditionally, there have been two opposed theories of the interpretation of myth, equally influential, one of which is broadly realist, in the sense defined above, and one of which is broadly non-realist. One assumes the perspective of perfection, translating narrative into the terms of truth, *mythos* into *logos*. The other sees myth as a matter of permanent possibility, trusting in the ongoing power of *mythos* itself. One is bound to a hierarchy; the other is open to a horizon. Moreover, while both are examples of what we are calling 'mythic reading', it is the latter which is the more conscious of itself as a mythopoeic activity. These two readings are 'allegory' and what we are calling 'radical typology'. The latter is in turn to be distinguished from 'orthodox typology', which is halfway between the two. It is only 'radical typology' which has a perpetual sense of horizon, involving an ongoing dialectic of the sacred and the profane.

ALLEGORY: THE PERSPECTIVE OF PERFECTION

Whoever Homer was, he would probably have been surprised had he encountered an allegorical reading of his own poetry. Allegory did not spring spontaneously from anything we might call 'the Greek mind'. But the fact that one particular interpretive practice did emerge in Hellenic culture should not be ignored. Here we will indicate how and why it developed, and what it involved.

We may infer that the poems known as the *Iliad* and the *Odyssey*, which reached their final form in the eighth century BC, offered to the Greeks of their time a useful summary of received myths, as well as recounting the history of their glorious past, focused on the Trojan War. But perhaps the most important thing about them is that they were, and are, sophisticated works of literary invention, involving impressive use of received formulas. These could be set phrases, such as 'rosy-fingered dawn'. They could be typical scenes, such as the arming of a warrior prior to battle. They could even be recurrent plot structures, such as the withdrawal of the greatest warrior from combat (in the case of the *Iliad*, Achilles), with all its dire consequences for his comrades in arms, followed by his triumphant re-engagement. It was this material which was embellished orally over the years, until it attained the written form which we know.

That form is usually known as epic. Though the word 'epic' (from the Greek, *epos*) may be defined as an oral narrative, which suggests an affinity to myth, we normally distinguish it from myth proper because its subject matter is historical humanity rather than divinity or superhuman heroism – though at many points it does have strong suggestions of the paradigm of hero myth. The main protagonist of the *Iliad* is Achilles, the warrior of formula who withdraws from combat only to return just in time to ensure victory. The protagonist of the *Odyssey* is, of course, Odysseus: having fought in the war, he returns home to his kingdom – encountering, again according to formula, various monsters and mishaps on the way. Achilles is characterised by his devastating wrath; Odysseus, a more subtle figure, is characterised by the ingenuity with which he escapes from perils. Either way the focus is on the human world, albeit a noble or regal one. Or, to put this the other way round, though the protagonists are mythic in the simplest sense (Achilles and Odysseus did not exist), they are presented as if historical, and so of intense human interest. The hero of epic is a noble warrior or king, and his business is the founding and destroying of cities – for instance, 'Ilium' (Troy) – and the affirmation of his own excellence in the face of imminent death. By virtue of his heroism he stands halfway between divinity and mere humanity; yet if he errs or offends against the higher, cosmic law, he must suffer, more terribly than any ordinary mortal. The protagonist of Homeric epic stands poised between the gods and ourselves. But unlike the protagonist of hero myth, he is always convincingly human. Thus, we are usually more interested in his exploits than in the activities on Mount Olympus, which provide a mere backdrop to the war or adventure on which we are invited to concentrate. The deities of Homer are, significantly, presented as vividly, sometimes ridiculously, anthropomorphic: they exhibit all the lust and greed, pettiness and spite, of which humans are capable. They shift their allegiances in the war according to whim, or decide to hinder the hero's progress because of some nurtured grievance. Such figures are hard to imagine as the object of reverence. They are primarily literary devices, which help to get the tale told.

The contrast here is with the *Theogony*, expressly written by Homer's contemporary Hesiod as an exposition of divine order, besides which human aspiration is made to seem a neglible matter. A literary elaboration on primitive creation myth, it celebrates the rise and triumph of Zeus, the sky father. Though the poem shows his authority being challenged – as by Prometheus, the Titan who steals fire from heaven on behalf of humanity – we also see it strongly reasserted. Providing the genealogy of cosmic rule, the *Theogony* effectively justifies the given social hierarchy. As Fritz Graf puts it, the story demonstrates that 'religious and cultural integration is what defines humanity' (Graf 1993: 86). Or, as Burke would say, in narrating 'principals' the poem consolidates 'principles'. However, it was Homer's apparent irreverence, not Hesiod's attempt at authorisation, which set the agenda for subsequent approaches to myth in Greece. If we take the evidence of fifth-century Athenian tragedy, we might say that myth was maintaining its hold on the popular mind but that the authority of the Olympian cosmos was beginning to be eroded. For instance, the tragedies of Euripides (480–406 BC) explored the problem of making sense of an apparently unpredictable and unfair universe. Indeed, he so frequently put into the mouth of his characters a critique of the gods that we cannot but infer a consistent authorial position. But then, Euripides' implicit enquiry was only echoing the explicit statement of the philosopher Xenophanes (570–475 BC), that Homer had 'attributed to the gods everything that is a shame and reproach among men, stealing and committing adultery and deceiving each other' (Kirk and Raven 1960: 168). This 'rational' approach to myth, as it is usually called, went further than any of Euripides' characters, in that it took the anthropomorphic nature of the gods to be a reason for rejecting myth itself. For the truth which Xenophanes sought was transcendent; myth, with its naive projection of human qualities onto supposedly higher beings, simply got in the way. The medium was obscuring the message. Xenophanes wanted a religious meaning beyond mere narrative.

This kind of thinking was significant as part of a general process of demythologization. Increasingly after the fifth century BC the power of Greek myth diminished in the face of Greek philosophical speculation. Even those sympathetic to the old gods, and even those engaged in writing narrative poems themselves, effectively undermined the aura of their mythic material. In about 300 BC Euhemerus of Messene wrote his *Sacred Document*, recounting a voyage to an island where the secret of the gods' origins was waiting to be discovered. Zeus, it transpired, had originally been a human hero who was deified by the community in return for his ousting of tyrants from the vicinity. The term 'Euhemerism' is still used for any mythography which explains away myth as 'merely' historical. Despite the reverent intentions of the *Sacred Document*, its influence was negative: if Zeus had once existed in history, as a mortal, and was subsequently turned into a deity by human will, then the aura of the founding narratives had been effectively diminished.

The line running from the 'rational' to the 'Euhemeristic' constituted the negative aspect of Greek mythography, by which myth was thereby drained of its power. It is perhaps possible to allocate the philosopher Plato (428–348 BC) to this same process. When, in his most famous philosophical dialogue, *The Republic*, he had his mentor Socrates regretfully banish the poets from his ideal state, Homer and Hesiod were not exempted. Like Xenophanes before him, Plato subordinated narrative to reason, human-made myth to transcendent truth. If the citizens of the republic were to fall under the spell of 'the sweetened Muse', then 'pleasure and pain will be enthroned in your city instead of law and the principle which the community accepts as best in any given situation' (Russell and Winterbottom 1972: 74).

Yet it would misrepresent Plato to say that he simply rejected narrative *mythos* in favour of rational *logos*. Rather, his attitude was deeply ambivalent. To appreciate this, we must clarify his general philosophical position briefly. He posited a timeless world of what he called 'the Forms': that is, universal essences. They alone were real, so that to call someone good or something beautiful was to say that they reflected, in their own inferior fashion, that higher realm in which the Good and pure Beauty resided. Plato opposed the eternal order of being (above) to the temporal chaos of becoming (below). Thus his position was what Cupitt calls traditional or 'metaphysical realism' – or again, given its rigidly hierarchical thinking, 'ladder realism' (Cupitt 1986: 43). However, gestures could be made from the lower realm to the higher. Or rather, truth could be made palatable by being embellished in the inferior mode of narrative; designed as it was to please the senses, it could yet serve the intellect. Thus Plato's dialogues themselves are most vividly remembered for Plato's own fables. *The Republic* itself contains the story of the cave, a curious variation on hero myth. It depicts the world of sensual experience as a dark underground cavern, the inhabitants of which take flickering firelit images to be reality. One day one of their number escapes and sees the sun for the first time. The hero, that is, is the philosopher, who is able to transcend our illusory world by the power of contemplation and reason.

Essentially, what we have in this tale is an allegory. That is what happened to Greek myth once it had been demythologized, as Xenophanes had already done by the time Plato recounted the myth of the cave and as Euhemerus would do a century or so later. Allegory was the positive aspect of the same process. Where they explained away the power of myth, reducing it to anthropomorphism and 'mere' history, Plato allowed it its place in the larger scheme of rational understanding. For him the philosophical meaning preceded the myth, and the myth's interest resided in its capacity to illustrate that meaning. The word 'allegory' comes from the Greek, *allos*, or 'other'. Allegorical tales are those which in effect announce, or are made to announce, their own intention: to say *this* in terms of *that*. Thus the 'other' is always subsumed under the 'same'. The narrative is not allowed to exceed the argument; the medium is not allowed to exceed the message. Allegory is domesticated myth. Thus Homer himself was rendered safe, so to speak, in the centuries following Plato. The text was translated into the manageable terms of a presupposed meaning. This could be philosophical, but also theological. Indeed, Christianity was particularly interested in taming Homer. While the early church fathers found the negative Euhemeristic approach to Greek myth useful, since it exposed the Greek deities as glorified mortals, it also made the most of allegory, since it positively demonstrated that even benighted pagans could appreciate the necessity for moral instruction. Homer had not been able to benefit from Christ's redemption, but his narratives had glimmerings of Christian truth – obscured, of course, by all the absurd, or even demonic, antics of the Olympian gods and goddesses. Beyond the narrative lay the theological and moral essence, the transcendent truth, the allegorical meaning. This mode of mythography survived the middle ages, despite the disappearance of the primary Homeric texts, to be revived with enthusiasm in the Renaissance. Searching through Graeco-Roman myths for Christian truths became something of an obsession. The Italian mythographer Natale Conti was perhaps typical when, in his *Mythologia* (1616), he read Odysseus' return to Ithaca as demonstrating that a wise Christian, patiently enduring hardships and avoiding temptation, would eventually live 'in his true fatherland, sharing with other men in the councils of God' (Allen 1970: 95). Myth had been tamed once and for all, or so it seemed.

RADICAL TYPOLOGY: PERMANENT POSSIBILITY

Allegory was only one aspect of early Christianity. The other was typology, which might be illustrated by reference to the New Testament itself. Here the role of such crucial figures from early Biblical myth as Adam and Moses is reaffirmed and yet also rewritten. To St Paul, Jesus is the 'second' Adam, restoring the paradisal bliss lost in the original fall from the garden of Eden. For 'as in Adam all died, so in Christ all shall be made alive' (I Corinthians 15: 22). Moses, hero of the earliest myth of deliverance, anticipates Jesus more positively, and in at least three ways. John Ferguson explains:

> First, because he was the instrument of the first great act of liberation; the Messiah would re-enact the act of liberation. Second, because he was associated with the Old Covenant, as Jesus with the New, in which Law found its fulfilment in love. Third because Moses striking the rock so that water gushed out formed the living emblem of Jesus giving the Living Water (John 4.7–13).
>
> (Ferguson 1980: 99)

In each case, the former person or event provides the 'type', which carries with it its special promise; the latter provides the 'anti-type', which does not constitute the opposite of the type, despite the unusual prefix, but rather its realisation. The type is the pre-figurement; the anti-type is the fulfilment. The whole of the Bible is taken to point forward to the triumph of Jesus Christ over death. Typology is the myth of deliverance turned into a foolproof mode of mythography.

The first, correct impression of this kind of mythic reading is that it is an arrogant act of appropriation. A whole body of scripture and belief – the Judaic, which already comprehends the Israelite and the Hebrew – is translated at a stroke into a mere prologue to an upstart religion. It becomes an 'Old' Testament, foil to the 'New'. (The resonance of this hegemonic act is still with us in our very dating system, BC and AD, which is in itself evidence that the modern mind continues to think mythically.) But just as with apocalyptic myth there is a dynamic tension between the already and the not yet, so with the mythic reading known as typology we must distinguish between the orthodox and radical aspects.

Orthodox typology, which is implicit in the Epistles and Gospels, and which is explicit in the works of early church fathers such as Origen and Augustine, sees all promises as now fulfilled, with the Word having been incarnated into the darkness of this world and then having returned to heaven, its mission complete. Now it speaks to us through the hierarchy and authority of the church. In this sense typology is only a variation upon allegory, and is committed to traditional realism. Orthodox typology is wary of admitting the fantastic or legendary nature of the story of Jesus, or *mythos*, and wants to translate it into doctrine, or *logos*. For if the promises of the Old Testament have been finally and absolutely fulfilled in the New, then narrative is no more. That is, orthodox typology is a kind of demythologization.

But it is possible to extract the pattern of promise and fulfilment from that of scriptural completion, and see it working through and beyond the Bible. Peter Munz has suggested that typology is a valid mythic principle in its own right, and needs appreciating as such. 'Every myth we know', he declares, 'has both a past and a future' (Munz 1973: ix). The elements of myth that are called 'type' and 'anti-type' could, if rescued from orthodoxy, be taken as explicit indices of the way mythology works anyway. This is 'the phenomenon of historical seriality' (Munz 1973: xii). In other words, all myths presuppose a previous narrative, and in turn form the model for future narratives. Strictly speaking, the pattern of promise and fulfilment need never end; no sooner has one narrative promise been fulfilled than the fulfilment becomes in turn the promise of further myth-making. Thus myths remake other myths, and there is no reason why they should not continue to do so, the mythopoeic urge being infinite. This understanding is what we are calling radical typology. Where orthodox typology works in terms of closure, radical typology works in terms of disclosure.

If we allow that typology can occur both within and without the Bible, we can see that work as provisional, involving both an external and internal dynamic. Taking the external first: if we read carefully the opening of the Book of Genesis, written in the sixth century BC after the Israelites had been in exile in Babylon, then we can see that it is a deliberate attempt to go beyond the Babylonian myth of creation. For, where 'Enuma elish' envisages creation as coming about from the defeat by the young, male warrior god Marduk of the primal, female chaos monster Tiamat (from whose divided corpse he constructs the cosmos), Genesis envisages creation as being effected by Yahweh all at once, out of nothing. The earlier myth, which assumes an initial polytheism, is thereby superseded; monotheism is asserted. But the persistence of that myth becomes evident when we consider that the idea of creation out of nothing is very difficult to articulate and maintain. The very language of the first chapter of Genesis suggests that Yahweh is doing battle with some force or other, notably the formless 'deep'. Moreover, the Hebrew name for 'the deep', over which the spirit of Yahweh is said to move, is etymologically related to the Babylonian 'Tiamat'. The old cosmology lingers between the lines of the new narrative; myth is hidden within myth. Yet the triumph is indubitable: Genesis is no mere footnote to 'Enuma elish'. Thus there is a tension in typology: the anti-type is dependent upon the type; yet the anti-type manages to evade its debt to the type.

So much is similarly evident when we consider the internal dynamic within the Bible itself. The last, Christian book totally rewrites the first, Judaic book. Genesis gives us the creation, the garden of Eden, Adam and Eve, and the tempting serpent (itself obviously owing something to the chaos dragon Tiamat). Revelation gives us 'a new heaven and a new earth', the garden-city of Jerusalem, the Messiah and his bride, and the lamb who overthrows both dragon and beast. The latter text makes no sense without the former, since re-creation presupposes creation, just as salvation presupposes the fall. But the former text has been, in effect, rewritten as a prologue to the apocalypse. There again, if this internal dynamic is inseparable from the wider project of making and remaking myth, we need not take the achievement of Revelation as final. Indeed, as we have seen, the rhetoric of that work speaks out of a sense of crisis, transition and instability; informed by a past promise, it projects, from a present of oppression, a future of liberation. The apocalypse is always now, but that now is always involved in an ongoing dialectic. Thus the apocalyptic myth, while available for orthodox recuperation, as in Spenser's *The Fairie Queene*, can never finally be domesticated, but will always invite radical reaffirmation, as in Winstanley's *Fire in the Bush*.

According to Erich Auerbach, typology, or 'figural interpretation', of its very nature 'differs from most of the allegorical forms known to us by the historicity both of the sign and what it signifies' (Auerbach 1984: 54). But this assessment may be misleading unless we recall the distinction made above, between orthodox and radical typology. Indeed, we should be aware that many 'figural' interpreters have tried to tame Biblical myth, constraining its 'historicity'. Hence we need to rescue typology from its orthodox proponents, and affirm its radical potential. Myths work according to the imperative of narrative dynamism and will always evade the stasis of doctrine. Thus the premature finality of realism is the death of myth; the not yet of apocalypse becomes, then, the key to mythic life.

One mythic thinker who resisted finality was Joachim, twelfth-century abbot of Fiore. He projected a global history based on the Holy Trinity, inspired by his reading of Revelation. He envisaged a sequence of three ages: the first *status* (Latin, 'state', 'situation', 'stance') was that of the Father; the second was that of the Son; the third, which was to come, was that of the Spirit. Joachim's visionary, threefold scheme is summed up by Marjorie Reeves as follows:

> the first *status* was under the law, the second *status* under grace, the third *status*, which we expect soon, will be under a more ample grace; . . . the first was lived in the servitude of slaves, the second in the servitude of sons, but the third will

> be in liberty; . . . the first was lived in fear, the second in faith, the third will be in love; the first was the *status* of slaves, the second of sons, but the third will be that of friends; the first of old men, the second of young men, the third of children; the first was lived in starlight, the second in the dawn, the third will be the perfect day.
>
> (Reeves 1976: 14)

It should be stressed that it was essential to Joachim's belief in 'the fruition of history' that the agencies to bring the church through the transition period to the third age must be human, albeit divinely inspired (Reeves 1976: 29). Indeed, the 'everlasting gospel' announced in Revelation 16: 6 was going to express the freedom of a new 'Spiritual Intelligence' possessed by men and women.

Thus Joachim's triadic scheme of the three ages, of Father, Son and Holy Ghost, is both a valid, post-Biblical myth in its own right and a good example of what we are calling radical typology. For, taking his cue from Revelation, he refuses to accept the closure of fulfilment: that is, he follows the logic of type and anti-type to the point where both are subsumed in a dialectic of infinite potential:

> the reign of love on this earth, love from the heart, can dispense with the law of both Testaments; Judgement Day is indefinitely postponed and its awesome sting is removed by the transitional third stage of the Holy Ghost. The great expectation for which Joachim prepares the faithful is not the end of the world and a transcendent resolution in Heaven, but . . . the appearance . . . of the Holy Ghost on earth.
>
> (Manuel 1965: 38–9)

This third age of the spirit will be expressed by a 'Third Testament'. The product of the profane imagination, it will supersede even the proclamations of Christ.

One author who may be seen as having attempted to draw up his own 'Third Testament' is the Italian poet Dante Alighieri (1265–1321). Here we will consider the text which became known as *The Divine Comedy*, but which was known by its author simply as 'The Comedy'. We will take it to be a secular 'anti-type' to the whole of the Bible, and we will take it to be a major mythopoeic work. In order to do that we must bear in mind what was said above about the dynamic context of the Biblical myth.

If orthodox typology involves a thorough rewriting of scripture, radical typology involves a shift of emphasis from the sacred to the profane. While it may appear to be arrogant appropriation, similar to that by which one set of scriptures becomes a foil to another, its effect is to liberate the imagination. Its business is not dogmatic assertion but narrative exploration. Dante's *Divine Comedy* (1314–21) may be taken to exemplify it. It is not only an extension of Biblical myth, it is a unique mythopoeic achievement. It creates not one but three 'unprecedented worlds': those of the *Inferno*, the *Purgatorio* and the *Paradiso*. Though derived from scriptural hints, in detail they are uniquely Dante's invention. Here we will briefly summarise the plot which contains them. Midway through his life, the narrator dreams that he has lost his way in a dark wood. The Roman classical poet Virgil appears, offering to escort him through hell and purgatory, from where he can proceed to heaven itself. Hell is conceived as a conical tunnel, reaching to the centre of the earth. Various categories of sinners are assigned to the nine infernal circles, where they receive appropriate punishments. At the very bottom is Satan himself. Passing him by, Dante and Virgil find their descent becoming an ascent, and they eventually reach the opposite surface of the earth. There is located the foot of the mountain of purgatory: this is the place where the souls of the dead are purged of their sins before admittance to heaven. The two pilgrims encounter various groups of repentant sinners on the seven circular ledges of the mountain. On its summit lies the earthly paradise, or the garden of Eden, where

Dante meets none other than Beatrice, the woman he admires more than any. As she approaches, a hundred angels sing '*Benedictus qui venis!*': that is, 'Blessed are thou that comest', which is only a slightly modified version of Matthew 21: 9: 'Blessed is He who cometh' (Dante 1995: 364–5). Virtually the same words are applicable to both Christ and Beatrice. Her importance could not be greater. Indeed, Dante stands trembling in adoration before her. Virgil, as a pre-Christian pagan, can serve as guide no longer, and it is Beatrice who conducts Dante through heaven. As hell was divided into circles, so heaven is divided into spheres: those of the moon, of Mercury, Venus, the sun, Mars, Jupiter, Saturn, the fixed stars, and the '*primum mobile*' or first mover. The spheres are in ascending order of merit, and he is conducted through them by Beatrice. The journey culminates in a vision of the divine light itself, which is the primary expression of 'the Love that moves the sun and the other stars' (Dante 1995: 585).

This grand narrative, culminating in a vision of perfection, while obviously indebted to Christian doctrine, is original and powerful enough to be recognised as a myth in its own right. Over the centuries, however, the myth has been systematically tamed by orthodox interpretation. Again and again, it has been defined and read as an allegory. After all, it depicts the progress of the human soul from error and ignorance to the contemplation of God. It comprises a journey through three eternal realms: hell, purgatory and heaven. The poet's guide through the first two, Virgil, might allegorically stand for classical reason. Regarding Beatrice, we might say that reason, while valid, can only take us so far, and that she represents the ultimate power of Christian grace. Read in this way, the poem becomes a monumental justification of medieval order. Its vertical journey, in which the protagonist–poet acquires the wisdom of humility as he ascends nearer and nearer to God, articulates the need for submission to hierarchical authority. However, the *Comedy* is such a richly imaginative work that when reading it we always sense the narrative power exceeding any neatly paraphrasable meaning. Certainly, more recent commentary on the poem has dwelt on the enigma of the *mythos* rather than seeking out directly the certainty of the *logos*.

Thomas Altizer, following the logic of Dante's narrative, celebrates his 'heresy'. For him the presence of Joachim is vital, and he sees Dante as dramatically influenced by the abbot's secularisation of sacred revelation and his affirmation, against St Augustine, of the 'City of Man' as equal to the 'City of God'. Thus the *Comedy* is 'the first Christian and apocalyptic epic', fusing history and heaven. It effects 'the transcendence of eternity in time itself, as time once again becomes an eschatological time, a time in which eternity is here and now'. Altizer explains:

> Now time itself is simultaneously an earthly and chronological time and a sacred and eternal time, a simultaneity revealed in the very chronology of the *Commedia*. For its epic action occurs during Eastertide in the year 1300 and lasts just a week, from the night of Maundy Thursday when Dante finds himself astray in the Dark Wood, until noon on the Wednesday after Easter, when Dante is transfigured in Heaven. The period of Dante's descent into Hell repeats and renews the time of Christ's death and burial, just as his journey through Purgatory renews and repeats the time of Christ's entombment, and his entrance into Paradise coincides with the dawn of Easter Sunday.
>
> (Altizer 1985: 123)

Thus Altizer confirms that Dante's vast, visionary work constitutes an approximation to Joachim's 'Third Testament'. It rewrites Christian myth in secular terms, and opens up a whole new world of promise. The 'coincidence of opposites', where the sacred and the profane meet, is not a distant goal but a present possibility. We might concur with Erich Auerbach in calling the form in which Dante achieves this dialectical vision 'figural realism', but only if we understand 'realism' as the realisation of the sacred in the profane, and forget all notions of a truth external to language, history and myth (Auerbach 1968: 196).

The poem's positive focus is the figure of Beatrice, who is not merely an aspect of Mary, mother of God, but ultimately 'the one and only avenue of salvation' for the poet (Altizer 1985: 127). Pushing this argument further, and recalling the benediction in the earthly paradise, we might conclude that Beatrice is as important to the poem as Christ himself – perhaps more so. Heretical as this sounds, it is not entirely misleading. Dante's audacious glorification of this female figure is consistent with Joachim's radical typology, and what we have said about the temporal dynamic of Biblical myth. We recall that in 'Enuma elish' creation was only achieved through the violent suppression of a she-monster. In Genesis, at the beginning of the Old Testament, this battle remained implicit in the creation story, but became explicit in the subsequent story of the fall, in which the first human female was associated with a serpent who would in time be identified as Satan. In Revelation, at the end of the New Testament, the defeat was announced of another demonic female, the 'whore of Babylon', whose power derived from that same serpent or dragon. Now, in this 'Third Testament', not only is the balance redressed by giving Mary her due as the agent by which the Messiah comes into the world, but the bounds of dogma are overleaped entirely by making a female figure who is of no theological significance, except to Dante, the main focus of redemption. If allegory presupposes an act of demythologization, radical typology proposes an act of remythologization. The sacred may be realised in the profane. The apocalypse may inform every moment of history.

ENLIGHTENMENT AND COUNTER-ENLIGHTENMENT

In the ancient and medieval eras the hierarchy of allegory was tempered by the historicity of typology; beyond both stretched the infinite horizon of radical typology, which still persists. Less dramatically, but still significantly, in early modernity the Enlightenment, which glorified reason and truth, was met by the counter-Enlightenment, which reaffirmed the power of imagination and myth. Here we will give the broad outline of this antithesis, in order to prepare ourselves for assessing the mythic readings of our own era. Radical typology will not be forgotten, but reaffirmed in a variety of settings.

In situating allegory, we had to consider two other kinds of mythography: the 'rational', which explained away myth as an inferior way of representing transcendent truth; and the 'Euhemeristic', which explained away myth as the deifying of historical figures. Both together comprised the negative aspect of allegory itself. Where they broke down the mythic material, allegory put it together again, but by now that material had effectively been deprived of its power. Similarly, when we come to the European Enlightenment, we find the same double-bind at work. Again, we will take one stage at a time. The 'rational' approach may be represented by Pierre Bayle (1647–1706), who in his *Historical and Critical Dictionary* equated 'myth' with 'absurdity' (Graf 1993: 14). The context of this usage should not be overlooked. For if it was in or around 1700 that modern mythography began, then it did so in a spirit of hostility to the very material it sought to explain. In particular, we might note that exploratory voyages to Africa and North America in the sixteenth and seventeenth centuries had suggested embarrassing parallels between contemporary 'savage' customs and the very myths that Renaissance scholars had been gleaning for signs of moral wisdom. Thus the distinction was introduced between archaic Greek myth (any narrative which was uncomfortably obscene or violent) and classical Greek literature (any narrative which pleased the enlightened mind). Reinforcing this rational approach was an equally modern version of Euhemerism. In *The Natural History of Religion*, the philosopher David Hume (1711–76) argued that myth was the origin of religion, and that both were founded in primitive humanity's fear of its environment. Terrified by any unfamiliar object in its surroundings, it had converted it into a sacred being – a god or goddess. Thus had the worship of natural objects begun. Thereafter, it had seemed only fitting to deify extraordinary men and women, just as Euhemerus argued.

Though the scholar of Greek mythology, Fritz Graf, argues that the Enlightenment was averse to the allegorisation of myth, it is possible to discover something like allegory complementing the negative views of Bayle and Hume. For example, though Christian Gottlob Heyne (1729–1812), who had formed his ideas about myth by about 1760, agreed with Hume that it expressed a primitive terror, he thought the very nature of the expression might repay serious study. For the concrete, sensuous language of myth, though crude, had led to the subtle delights of poetry. Myth was a product of the childhood of humanity, but as such it could afford insights into our origins. Myth was the primary content; poetry was the secondary form. The method required to discover the content underlying the form was philology, the historical and comparative science of language. In the case of Greece, the myths had come down to us in complex and sometimes contradictory ways: for example, Homeric epic and Athenian tragedy. The task was to work one's way back beyond both to discover the original material. Thus we could begin to understand the essential Greek mind in its linguistic context. It is possible, then, to see Heyne's approach as allegorical, working upon the narrative or *mythos* in two retrospective stages (first form, then content) until it delivered the hidden meaning he sought.

It is through Heyne that we can intuit the positive mythographic interest of the Enlightenment, such as it was. Thus, though archaic myth-making was understood to be immature compared to modern rationality, it could not simply be left behind. Moreover, though ancient Greek literature had derived from archaic Greek myth, it was clearly of interest as an example of emergent clarity. The Enlightenment in the main celebrated classical Greece without reservation, withholding approval only from the dark centuries preceding it. This darkness was considered to have been interrupted only by the light of the occasional poet such as Homer, provided he had been suitably allegorised first.

As with Plato, the allegorical principle of the late seventeenth and early eighteenth centuries was reason. *Logos* set out to explain *mythos*. But now it went much further. As Peter Docherty explains: 'The Enlightenment aimed at human emancipation from myth, superstition and enthralled enchantment to mysterious powers and forces of nature through the progressive operations of critical reason.' This solution, however, turned out to create its own problems. 'In the desire to contest any form of animistic enchantment by nature, Enlightenment set out to think the natural world in an abstract form.' Thus it could only 'think' that which could be systematized. 'In a word, reason has been reduced to . . . a specific *form* of reason. More importantly, this specific inflection of reason is also now presented as if it were reason-as-such, as if it were the only valid or legitimate form of rational thinking.' What offered itself as emancipation turned out to be suppression. Docherty quotes Adorno and Horkheimer's *Dialectic of Enlightenment* (1944): 'Enlightenment behaves toward things as a dictator toward men. He knows them in so far as he can manipulate them.' Reason, that is, became power; and power could only function by having an 'other' to suppress, whether nature, human beings (as 'savages') or myths (Docherty 1993: 7–8).

However, in the very act of demystifying traditional myths, the Enlightenment was engaged in its own mythic enterprise. We have already referred to the 'myth of mythlessness'. Now we can go further, and take into account Jean-François Lyotard's proposition that the Enlightenment invented two modern 'metanarratives', which have held good up to the present era. The first, particularly strong in France, and finding dramatic expression in the French Revolution, is that of 'the liberation of humanity'. The second, particularly strong in Germany, and finding more refined but no less ambitious expression in the writings of Georg Wilhelm Friedrich Hegel (1770–1831), is that of 'the speculative unity of all knowledge'. Each of these grand narratives of modernity has its own ideal protagonist: the 'hero of liberty', or activist, and the 'hero of knowledge', or philosopher (Lyotard 1984: 31). The paradox of both narratives is that, though dedicated to *logos* – aiming to transcend error, whether perceived as injustice or as ignorance, in the name of reason – they by definition exemplify the need for *mythos*. Unfortunately, Lyotard has since confused the issue by suggesting that, though the 'metanarratives' of modernity clearly derive from Christianity, they are not myths as such since 'they look for legitimacy not in an original founding act but in a future to be accomplished' (Lyotard 1992: 29). This is to ignore the very dynamic of the Biblical myth of deliverance, which comprehends both creation (founding) and apocalypse (future). That said, his overall case remains valid, that these 'metanarratives' only work provided they are taken as non-narrative truth, the conviction being that the Enlightenment is an end which justifies the means. That is, it remains valid as the expression of a universal law, whatever or whoever is suppressed in the name of its progress.

It was this facile assumption of non-narrative truth that provoked what Isaiah Berlin calls the counter-Enlightenment. If there was such a movement, and if it had a founder, then that title must go to Giambattista Vico (1688–1744). An inspiration to a writer we have already considered, James Joyce, he refused to see myth as error, and insisted that it was an early, necessary and wholly admirable phase in the development of civilisation. In his *The New Science* he argued that the only 'science' of humanity which could be of use was one that comprehended what lay behind *logos*. Not reason but imagination was the key to myth. Myth was not a failed attempt to articulate rational truth but was the creative impulse underlying human history. Primitive mythopoeia was the source of all experience and all expression. If it represented the childhood of humanity, that was no reason to treat it with condescension. Far from patronising it, the modern age should be trying to understand how it had informed its own character and ideas. Vico, according to Joseph Mali, achieved the 'rehabilitation of myth':

> he saw that in our (and any other) civilization the fictions of mythology illuminate the 'real world' by constituting or 'prefiguring' all its human actions and institutions: unlike natural occurrences which display law-like, repetitive regularities which are unknowable to us because they are totally alien to our form of life, human occurrences throughout history display forms of action which are knowable to us insofar as we can recognize in them the coherent narrative patterns of the mythical stories with their well-made characters and plots.
>
> (Mali 1992: 3–4)

That is, myth shapes history, and therefore it shapes culture. The religious beliefs, social customs and linguistic commonplaces of each age are reaffirmations of, and elaborations upon, primitive mythic patterns. Thus what characterises the counter-Enlightenment, as represented by Vico, is not the allegory of reason but the typology of imagination. As Peter Munz explains:

> In Platonic thought and in every philosophy that was derived from it, there had been an unbridgeable gulf between time and Idea, the particular and the universal, becoming and being. The gulf remained unbridgeable even when modern evolutionist thinking reversed Plato's evaluation of it. Plato had believed that truth was on the side of the Idea and that becoming was a form of illusion. Modern evolutionism stood Plato on his head; but the dichotomy remained. Vico's explanation eliminated the gulf. The Truth of Idea depended on the temporal extension of the typological series.
>
> (Munz 1973: 120–3)

That is, *mythos* precedes and informs *logos*. Without Homer there can be no Plato. The profane imagination expresses itself initially through mythic narrative; the principles of philosophy, far from being eternal, are the result of a long process of reflection on, reaction to and rewriting of that initial imaginative expression. They form the anti-type to its type. Time produces the 'Idea', imagination produces 'Truth', the profane produces the sacred.

The typology of imagination was, it might be said, the inspiration of the Romantic poet William Blake (1757–1827). Putting all his effort into revitalising the Christian myth, it was he who in 1820 called the Bible 'the Great Code'. But far from seeing that book of books as a constraining presence, he felt able to rewrite it totally, in the belief that 'Eternity is in love with the productions of time' (Blake 1971: 151). Thus instead of setting out from the idea of an omniscient and omnipotent God who had created the cosmos and then created humanity, he saw humanity as the source of both cosmos and creator. That is, long before Hegel proposed, and Nietzsche confirmed, the 'death of God', Blake had comprehended that very principle within a new, radical Christianity. The God of the Old Testament, whom he also identified with the abstract, inhuman deity of the Enlightenment, he called 'Urizen' (the product of 'your reason'). Moreover, according to his dramatic rewriting of the New Testament, that God – who had never existed in the first place, except as a human projection – could be said to have died once and for all with the birth of Jesus. The God of the New Testament had freed us from the obligation to worship a deity distinct from ourselves. Moreover, if 'Empire' – the tyranny of Urizen – was 'against Art', then Jesus was the greatest of 'Artists': 'The Old & New Testaments are the Great Code of Art. Art is the Tree of Life. God is Jesus' (Blake 1971: 777). In other words, false religion was the dogma that enslaved; true religion was the story that liberated. But meanwhile, Christianity went on clinging to its arid and abstract sky-father and opposing sacred truth to profane imagination.

Blake, then, has his own myth to recount: a rewriting and fusion of the creation and deliverance paradigms. But his particular genius is to remain faithful to the form of his 'Great Code' while turning its world, as far as the orthodox are concerned, upside down. *Songs of Innocence* (1789), with its comforting, apparently stable imagery of shepherd and lamb, father and child, forms the conventional prologue to this radical myth, which begins with *The Marriage of Heaven and Hell* (1793). Here he demonstrates that ostensibly stark opposites such as heaven and hell, good and evil, reason and desire, always turn out to be dialectical 'contraries', without which 'there is no progression'. In order to redress the balance against orthodoxy, the *Marriage* commends the wisdom of the 'devils': 'Energy is eternal delight . . . . The road of excess leads to the palace of wisdom . . . . What is now proved was once only imagined . . . . Exuberance is Beauty . . . . Where man is not, nature is barren.' Humanity has repressed this wisdom because it has forgotten that 'All deities reside in the human breast.' It is as if 'man has closed himself up, till he sees all things thro' narrow chinks of his cavern.' He has come to regard the very limits he has set himself as eternal and immutable. The alternative, which we have already encountered in our discussion of Jim Morrison, is clear: 'If the doors of perception were cleansed every thing would appear to man as it is, infinite' (Blake 1971: 150–4). Hence in the poem 'London' from *Songs of Experience* (1794) we learn that it is 'the mind-forg'd manacles' which keep humanity subject to state and church hierarchy (Blake 1971: 216). If 'all deities reside in the human breast', then so do all oppressive doctrines. In *The First Book of Urizen*, published the same year as *Experience*, the Book of Genesis is rewritten so that the creation of our cosmos turns out to have been simultaneous with the fall. For if the world we know is the result of Urizen's having separated himself out from a primal harmony known as eternity, and if Urizen, like all deities, is human in origin, an aspect of our own minds, then to find ourselves in this world of false laws and limits is effectively to have restricted our own vision. Letting reason take over from our other faculties, we have become alienated – or 'fallen'. We have constructed a false ideal, have come to believe in a tyrannous perfection: 'One King, one God, one Law' (Blake 1971: 224).

We move beyond this fallen world, with its sterile antithesis of innocence and experience, in Blake's notes to *Vala, or The Four Zoas* (1795–1804): 'Unorganiz'd Innocence' is, we are told, 'An Impossibility' (Blake 1971: 380). There is, we understand, a third realm beyond the two worlds of the *Songs*: an innocence that is 'organized', that synthesises what are now recognised as contraries. Again, he elaborates upon his 'Great Code'. In the Bible the 'innocence' of the garden of Eden is lost, to be replaced by the 'experience' of the desert, wilderness or demonic city. Only then may Jerusalem, the heavenly city which is also a garden containing the lost tree of life, be attained and appreciated. Blake infers that the unfallen and the fallen worlds, as inner dispositions, presuppose one another. Thus the task of the imagination is to forge out of the contraries that third realm of 'organized innocence'. In the 'Preface' to *Milton* (1810) the poet, as bard, declares that he 'will not cease from Mental Fight' until 'we have built Jerusalem/In England's green and pleasant Land' (Blake 1971: 481). If we were ever in any doubt, we now see that Blake is a visionary in the tradition of Joachim:

> Rouze up, O young Men of the New Age! Set your foreheads against the ignorant Hirelings! For we have Hirelings in the Camp, the Court & the University, who would, if they could, for ever depress Mental & prolong Corporeal War . . . . We do not want either Greek or Roman Models if we are but just & true to our own Imaginations, those Worlds of Eternity in which we shall live for ever and ever in Jesus our Lord.
>
> (Blake 1971: 480)

Blake's radical Christian myth is typological, since it draws on the

Bible in order to rewrite it; and it is apocalyptic, since it foresees the overthrow of those who have served Babylon. It invites the reader to abandon the Hellenic, allegorical distinction between eternity and time, and through the power of imagination end the state of alienation. That state, manifest in 'Corporeal War', has its source in mental oppression. Only by 'Mental Fight' may the heavenly city be built on earth.

The potentially infinite power of humanity is represented in his last major work *Jerusalem* (1804–20) by the figure of Albion, who is simultaneously England and the primal, universal man. He is woken from his long and heavy slumbers by Los, the artist, 'the Prophet of Eternity'. Albion realises that God, the cosmos, heaven and hell, the worlds of innocence and experience, and the whole of history, are all products of his own mind. Having realised this, he is able to meet Jesus as an equal and as a friend. The latter appears – appropriately, since he too is an 'Artist' – in the likeness of Los. Jesus is, ultimately, Albion's waking self, and his resurrected body may therefore be identified with the body of a newly risen humanity, open to imagination and love.

Blake's mythopoeic urge is firmly centred on the human mind rather than the external world of nature and cosmos. Myth is reaffirmed in an expressive rather than an explanatory spirit. Indeed, we might say that with Blake it becomes possible to believe that not only nature and cosmos but also society itself are external manifestations of the psyche. Hence hierarchy is above all an inner construction. Oppression is repression. In this respect there is a deep continuity between Romanticism and psychoanalysis. And it is to the latter movement that we now turn.

5

PSYCHE

THE PRIMAL CRIME

The word 'psyche' comes from a Greek word meaning 'breath' or 'life', and by extension 'soul'. The myth of Cupid and Psyche, originally Greek, features prominently in *The Golden Ass* by Apuleius, a Roman writer of the late second century BC. The story is as follows. Psyche is a beautiful maiden enamoured of Cupid, the god of love (the equivalent of the Greek Eros). He visits her every night but departs before sunrise, not having let her see him. But curiosity gets the better of her, and one night she lifts up her lamp to catch a glimpse of her lover; a drop of hot oil falls on his shoulder, and he awakes and flees. The abandoned Psyche wanders far and wide in search of Cupid. She becomes the slave of Venus (the Roman equivalent of Aphrodite, whom we have already met in our discussion of Frazer); the goddess imposes impossible tasks on her and treats her cruelly. Eventually, however, she is reunited with her lover and becomes immortal.

What fascinated Sigmund Freud (1865–1939) about this story was the implicit identification of the soul with sexuality, and the implicit identification of sexuality with conflict. Indeed, it might be said that the founder of psychoanalysis, drawing on what he had learnt about the human mind from the Romantics, made the implicit explicit, and in so doing radically revised the traditional understanding of the psyche. Marina Warner's entry on Freud, in her 'Short Dictionary of the Inner World', reads: 'Interpreter of dreams, story-teller, fantasist, hypnotist, mythographer, collector, reinvented the soul for C20' (Warner 1996: 41).

There are, however, two Freuds to contend with. There is firstly the heir of the Enlightenment, who equates religion with illusion and who confidently declares it possible to progress beyond the neurotic repetition compulsions which characterised primitive myth and ritual. This Freud is heavily influenced by Frazer. Like Frazer, he is a rationalist who sees myth as a kind of rudimentary error. For the one, its reliance on fertility magic means it is a false kind of science: killing the god was thought to effect a renewal of the crops, but the modern mind knows better. For the other, myth and religion are explained away once they have been recognised as neurotic. Like Frazer, he is an Euhemerist. For the one, the god was originally a king or magician, or at any rate a personage crucial to the well-being of the tribe. For the other, the god was the primal father deified. Again, like Frazer, he offers his own complementary allegory: where Frazer thinks the hidden meaning of myth lies in the cycle of vegetation, Freud thinks it lies in sex. This first Freud holds psychoanalysis to be a science, offering the one and only key to the mysteries of the unconscious. As our capacity for rational explanation of psychic drives expands, he tells us, so it will be possible to cure people of their neuroses. In other words, the Enlightenment metanarrative of emancipation holds good.

The second Freud, by contrast, is the heir of the counter-Enlightenment; it is he who answers to Warner's description. This Freud, while still thinking sex is the key to myth, is fully aware that his own ideas are provisional, narrative explorations of the soul rather than scientific truths. This is the man who, in conversation with Einstein towards the end of his life, goes so far as to question the very existence of objective veracity: 'It may perhaps seem to you as though our theories are a kind of mythology . . . . But does not every science come in the end to a kind of mythology?' (Freud 1950: 283). This is also the man who chooses as the epigraph for his *Interpretation of Dreams* (1900) a quotation from Virgil: 'If I cannnot move heaven, I will stir up the underworld.' Rational order can never, it seems, finally transcend the darkness of the unconscious.

It is this second, counter-Enlightenment Freud on which we will be concentrating. This is a figure who takes risks of inter-pretation, who radically rewrites the material he studies: in short, one who knows his 'science' to be 'a kind of mythology'. His source is *Oedipus Rex*, but he turns Sophocles' fifth-century Athenian drama into an exploration of repressed desire. Here is the background to the play, as summarised by Freud in *The Interpretation of Dreams*:

Oedipus, son of Laius, King of Thebes, and of Jocasta, was exposed as an infant because an oracle had warned Laius that the still unborn child would be his father's murderer. The child was rescued, and grew up as a prince in an alien court, until, in doubts as to his origin, he too questioned the oracle and was warned to avoid his home since he was destined to murder his father and take his mother in marriage. On the road leading away from what he believed was his home, he met King Laius and slew him in a quarrel. He came next to Thebes and solved the riddle set him by the Sphinx who barred his way. Out of gratitude the Thebans made him their king and gave him Jocasta's hand in marriage. He reigned long in peace and honour, and she who, unknown to him, was his mother bore him two sons and two daughters. Then at last a plague broke out and the Thebans made enquiry once

> more of the oracle. It is at this point that Sophocles' tragedy opens.
>
> (Freud 1974: 261)

And it is from this point that Sophocles begins his painstaking analysis of the conflict between reason and unacknowledged error. Not knowing himself to be the cause of the plague of Thebes, Oedipus is shown to be zealous in his efforts to discover the guilty one. It is only at the end that he realises that figure to be himself. Paul Ricoeur calls Sophocles' version of the myth a 'tragedy of truth', over which Freud has in turn transcribed a 'tragedy of sex' (Rée 1992: 39). The one is primarily interested in the dramatic convention of recognition, by which the protagonist is forced to face the consequences of his own actions, regardless of intention. The other is primarily interested in analysing repressed desires, hidden motives. He takes Sophocles' narrative as evidence that all male children experience a sexual trauma by which they desire the mother and detest the father, secretly wishing to commit incest and patricide. Thanks to Freud's radical rereading, it is now impossible to read the Athenian play about Oedipus (type) without thinking of the psychoanalytic theory of the Oedipus complex (anti-type).

The paradox and originality of Freud's typology, and what distinguishes him most from the Enlightenment, is that it looks backwards. Thus, contradicting the rational advocacy of emancipation from neurosis is the mythic fascination with what neurosis involves, namely the need to remember, return and repeat. Of course, this also distinguishes him from the radical visionaries so far discussed. In the typology of Joachim, Dante and Blake the present, while informed by past paradigms, is permanently open to the possibilities of the future. The apocalyptic moment is always just ahead, ready to suffuse the present with its power. It promises a new cosmos out of catastrophe. This is the *kairos*, the moment in which *chronos* is transformed. Freud believes in something like a *kairos*; but he places it in the past. 'The kairotic event has already happened' (Rieff 1951: 117). It is the time of sexual trauma, of the Oedipal complex. The present points not to a serene, rational future, as the Freud of the Enlightenment would believe, but rather backwards to a disturbing, irrational past. However, his *kairos* has its positive side. The story he tells of 'the primal crime' destabilises the present by throwing it into the long perspective of guilt, and so challenges us to reconsider our civilisation and our own lives. It has, perhaps, the same power, the same provocative effect, as Nietzsche's myth of eternal recurrence.

It is in *Totem and Taboo* (1913) that Freud develops his own myth. There we read that the founding event, decisive and irrevocable, was the Oedipal crime of the killing of the father. That is, the neurosis of the modern individual is a re-enactment of the collective guilt of 'the primal horde'. According to Freud, the first groups of human beings, existing in the latter part of the Old Stone Age, were patriarchal. The tribal patriarch appropriated all the women for himself. 'One day', as Freud puts it, in suitably fictional fashion, the other males, who were effectively his sons, 'came together, killed and devoured their father and so made an end of the patriarchal horde'. Now they had access to the females of the horde, their sisters. He goes on:

> Cannibal savages as they were, it goes without saying that they devoured their victim as well as killing him. The violent primal father had doubtless been the feared and envied model of each one of the company of brothers: and in the act of devouring him they accomplished their identification with him, and each one of them acquired a portion of his strength. The totem meal, which is perhaps mankind's earliest festival, would thus be a repetition and a commemoration of this memorable and criminal deed, which was the beginning of so many things – of social organization, of moral restrictions and of religion.
>
> (Freud 1985: 203)

Of course, this is not wholly original: the influence of Frazer is evident here. For one thing, father is to son as dying god is to reviving god. For another, the community is presented as gaining access to the patriarch's energy by means of magic. However, Freud's radical contribution is to introduce the psychological factor. The murder of the primal father induces such strong remorse that the group makes the patriarch its totem, associating him with a particular animal, here unspecified, to which it feels a special bond. The totemic meal, the eating of the animal in ritual fashion as if it were the father, has become the focus of the totemic clan, which replaces the primal horde. With the totem comes the taboo: a prohibition, for obvious reasons, against both patricide and incest. The logic of remorse leads to the revered totem-father becoming a god, and the totemic meal becoming a full-scale ritual. Human culture has begun, and with it, simultaneously, guilt, repression and religion.

Thus Freud looks backwards from the neurosis of the modern individual to the Oedipus myth; and then he looks further back, to 'the primal crime'. In order to understand the urge to remember, return and repeat, he does exactly what he sees his own patients doing. Thus his account of mythic thinking is itself mythic. Moreover, his myth is one that obliterates reassuring distinctions, most notably that between history and pre-history, and that between civilisation and savagery, as he orients all his evidence back to a founding sexual trauma. This runs the risk of being reductive, but the effect is more likely to be creatively disorienting. Sacred memory and sexual drive are played off against each other dialectically. There is always a further surprise in store. Thus in his last major work, *Moses and Monotheism: Three Essays* (1934–8), we find him going so far as to rewrite the Biblical myth of deliverance in terms of a repeated Oedipal struggle. The followers of Moses had, Freud conjectures, murdered him after the departure from Egypt. They had then decided to subscribe to monotheism, his favoured religious form, as a sign of remorse.

They adopted Yahweh, a local god, promoting him to the status of the one, universal God. Thus the Hebrew–Judaic faith became the religion of the father. But then, with the emergence of Christianity, for many Jews the crucified Jesus took the place of God the father, to whom St Paul believed him to have been sacrificed. The Christian faith centred on the son, not the father. Thus it was a reaffirmation, paradoxically, of the primal crime itself: though the starting point was the need to atone for humanity to God the father, it ended up glorifying the one who did the atoning. Later than Judaism, Christianity was effectively more retrogressive: it was more primal, more Oedipal, than the religion from which it had developed.

Situated in the perspective of both archaic past and living present, a more audacious rewriting of Biblical myth could not be envisaged – except perhaps Joachim's and Blake's. However, it has to be acknowledged that the Oedipal interest does not always lead Freud to produce absorbing literary criticism. His reading of *Hamlet* in *The Interpretation of Dreams*, for example, is notoriously crude and reductive. It may begin promisingly by presenting Shakespeare as reworking Sophocles' themes in an age when 'the secular advance of repression in the emotional life of mankind' leads to a greater 'indirectness' in treatment. But this awareness does not prevent Freud from going straight on to explain away the protagonist's actions – or, rather, failure to act. Hamlet's hesitation in killing the murderer of his father is, we are told, entirely due to a repressed desire to have done exactly the same thing. For Hamlet cannot bring himself to punish Claudius because he feels himself to be no better than the sinner whom he is supposed to condemn. Not content with thus dispelling the enigma of the play, Freud goes on to attribute its protagonist's complex to its author:

> it can of course only be the poet's mind which confronts us in *Hamlet*. I observe in a book on Shakespeare by Georg Brandes (1896) a statement that *Hamlet* was written immediately after

> the death of Shakespeare's father (in 1601), that is, under
> the immediate impact of his bereavement and, as we may well
> assume, while his childhood feelings about his father had been
> freshly revived.
>
> (Freud 1974: 265)

It is important to acknowledge the poverty of this, Freud's first attempt at interpreting Shakespeare's most famous work. Firstly, it reminds us how fine is the line which divides the two Freuds that we distinguished earlier. Indeed, in the course of the same volume, *The Interpretation of Dreams*, we find both the counter-Enlightenment myth-maker, who reads *Oedipus Rex* in the spirit of radical typology, and the Enlightenment rationalist, who explains away and reduces *Hamlet* in a perspective that is reminiscent of allegory. Secondly, it demonstrates that a mode of interpretation which may be daring and provocative in one instance may become dull and ponderous in another, if the sense of dynamism is lacking. For the whole point of radical typology is that making and reading myth should be part of an ongoing, narrative process and should not be nullified by mechanical and formulaic repetition. Once the Oedipal complex becomes a contrivance for slotting texts into place, then literary mythopoeia is effectively denied. Thirdly, the use of biographical information enforces the realist principle that the meaning of fictions are external to the workings of narrative. The fact of Shakespeare's father's death is used to rationalise, and so negate, the enigmatic power of the text.

A much more promising reading of *Hamlet*, which conveys his residual distrust of the Enlightenment cult of rationality, is given in his essay 'Psychopathic characters on the stage' (1906). Commenting on this, Jacqueline Rose reflects on the significance of Freud's use of a quotation from Lessing in connection with the play: 'A person who does not lose his reason under certain conditions can have no reason to lose':

Freud includes *Hamlet* in that group of plays which rely for their effect on the neurotic in the spectator, inducing in her or him the neurosis watched on stage, crossing over the boundaries between onstage and offstage and breaking down the habitual barriers of the mind. A particular *type* of drama, this form is none the less effective only through its capacity to implicate us *all*.

(Rose 1986: 43)

That is, 'instead of safely diagnosing Hamlet, his Oedipal drama, his disturbance, and subjecting them to its mastery and control', this radical interpretation 'turns back on to spectator and critic, implicating the observer in ... irrationality and excess' (Rose 1986: 43). Radical typology, the notion that we are all of us continually in the making, and that the certainty and stability of *logos* must always be put into doubt, here replaces the comfortably reductive allegory of the earlier reading.

It is ironic to note that Franz Kafka (1883–1924), another Jewish myth-maker, another visionary concerned to rewrite the legacy of father-centred religion, has suffered more than most writers from that kind of heavy-handed psychoanalysis, which Freud intermittently practised and inadvertently encouraged. It is as if his challenge and his mythopoeic power were so great that they needed defusing. Biographical explanation, crudely supported by Freudian concepts, thus saves us from having to acknowledge our own implication in his narratives:

His tortured relationship with his father appears to have been a dominating influence on his work ... His father – authoritarian, self-confident, bullying, philistine. Kafka – timid, sensitive and literary. 'In front of you,' Kafka wrote, 'I lost my self-confidence, and exchanged it for an infinite sense of guilt.'

Most of Kafka's stories and novels are about people who suffer, with no good reason, humiliation and chastisement.

(Jones and Handley 1988: 22)

To balance this kind of approach, we might cite W.H. Auden's judgement: 'Had one to name the author who comes closest to bearing the same kind of relation to our age as Dante, Shakespeare and Goethe bore to theirs, Kafka is the first one would think of.' George Steiner, confirming this judgement, adds that the power of the novels and stories evades biographical speculations, and concludes that Kafka's significance is that of a 'prophet'. His art is not merely personal; nor is it realistic. It is best described as 'transrealism', hallucinatory and terrifying: 'The key fact about Kafka is that he was possessed of a fearful premonition', that he saw 'the horror gathering'. Thus *The Trial* exhibits 'the classic model of the terror state'. It 'prefigures the furtive sadism, the hysteria which totalitarianism insinuates into private and sexual life, the faceless boredom of the killers' (Steiner 1969: 163).

Kafka criticism is perhaps the better for acknowledging this uncanny intuition of totalitarianism rather than attributing his creativity, in a reductive fashion, to an Oedipal trauma. For Kafka's fiction, while no doubt informed by anxiety concerning the author's father, is drastically diminished if we refuse to see it as anything more. It is how Kafka moves from this starting point to a full-scale interrogation of God the father and his project for humanity that should be the real focus of mythic interest. Again, though his recognition of sadism and sexual manipulation as necessary components of an oppressive regime is no doubt indebted to psychoanalysis, the latter cannot explain his power as 'prophet'. For ultimately, what marks him out as original is his radical relation to the legacy of the Law. Receiving it as a narrative which has hardened into a doctrine, Kafka sets out to remythologize it.

Moses was understood to have received the ten commandments, or decalogue, from Yahweh on Mount Sinai. These were, it transpired, designed to guide the Hebrews in their progress towards the promised land and the creation of the kingdom of Israel. With the division of the kingdom, and such catastrophes as the exile in Babylon, the need to observe the Law became more and more imperative, and it was hoped that if the people remained faithful to Yahweh's commandments, a divinely inspired ruler, or Messiah, would emerge to re-establish the kingdom once and for all. Waiting for this remained an essential part of traditional Judaic religion. Except for certain texts such as the Book of Daniel and except for certain immediately pre-Christian sects such as the Essenes, and unlike early Christianity, it expected a culmination of history rather than an apocalypse as such, with its radical disruption of chronological time. Kafka's genius was to take the act of waiting, now severed from its sacred dimension, as the clue to his own era.

The plot of his novel *The Trial* (1925) consists in the protagonist, Joseph K, being arrested without being accused of any specific crime. He keeps expecting to receive a proper charge and judgement. Finally, he is taken one evening by two nameless men to the edge of town and a knife held to his throat in a deserted stone quarry. At this moment, K looks across to the top window of a nearby house, from which a human figure leans out: 'Who was it? A friend? A good man? Someone who sympathized? Someone who wanted to help?' No help is at hand, however, and he dies, in his own last words, 'Like a dog!' (Kafka 1970: 250–1). The mythic power of the novel consists in the constant gestures it makes towards the idea of some ultimate Messianic moment, in which perspective all the bewilderment and agony of the protagonist might be situated and understood, only to deny us that possibility. All that is left is the individual, alone, alienated and afraid; and over and against him, an anonymous and destructive system.

Indeed, the heart of *The Trial* is itself a myth, but not one belonging to any distinct paradigm. This is the story of the doorway to the Law, which is told K by a priest he meets in the cathedral. The story is simple enough in form. A man comes to the doorway of the Law but the doorkeeper tells him he cannot admit him 'at this moment'. The man waits outside for days, for weeks, for months, for years. Finally, approaching death, he asks the doorkeeper why nobody else has ever come to the doorway, given that everybody 'strives to attain the Law'. The reply is: 'No one but you could gain admittance through this door, since this door was intended only for you. I am now going to shut it' (Kafka 1970: 236–7). We belittle the power of this myth if we label it, as many critics have done, as an allegory. For one thing, there is no code that can provide the answer to its mystery. It is not 'about' one particular theme or event. Rather, it is a terrifying parody of religious revelation, entirely appropriate to what Auden calls 'the age of anxiety'. For another thing, its effect is inseparable from radical typology. As with Freud, a legacy has been rewritten. In the Judaic scriptures, as in the Christian, there is an expectation of collective salvation: the kingdom will come. But here, the very promise of redemption has been both abstracted and atomised, and thereby negated. The Law is universal, indeed wholly imper-sonal, in its modern secular manifestation; but one lives, one is judged and one dies in isolation and absurdity. Kafka replaces the myth of deliverance with a myth of denial, and the hero myth with an anti-hero myth.

Further analysis of this central fable is not necessary here, but if one were to situate *The Trial* as a whole in literary terms, the obvious reference point would be Charles Dickens's *Bleak House* (1853). That novel traces the legal case of Jarndyce versus Jarndyce, which lasts so long that there is no estate left for the litigants once it is finished. Lives are wasted in the process, while the self-perpetuating bureaucracy of the Victorian legal system flourishes. We witness the oppression of the poor and the corruption of the rich. A massive work of great imaginative power, it comprises a denunciation of the workings of the demonic metropolis, the city ripe for destruction. Early in the novel, Miss Flite, a forlorn figure who keeps songbirds in a cage by her window, and who has been driven mad by a chancery case, informs the young wards of court, Richard and Ada, in the case of Jarndyce versus Jarndyce: 'I expect a judgment. Shortly. On the Day of

Judgment.' She adds that she has discovered that the sixth seal mentioned in the Book of Revelation is 'the Great Seal' of England (Dickens 1971: 81). The characters inhabit a London which seems identical with Babylon. And sure enough, this apocalyptic novel does place the demonic metropolis within the framework of the Biblical myth of deliverance. Chapter 1 begins with a vision of the city that parodies Genesis: 'As much mud in the streets, as if the waters had but newly retired from the face of the earth' (Dickens 1971: 49). At the end of Chapter 65, which is almost the last, the dying Richard tells Ada: 'I will begin the world!' And then comes the apocalyptic sign: 'at a late hour' the narrator Esther Summerson is visited by 'poor crazed Miss Flite', who tells her that she has 'given her birds their liberty' (Dickens 1971: 927).

Dickens's ending is, then, meant as a new beginning. A justice, which we might call divine but is probably better called poetic, is recognised and restored. The contrast with Kafka is extreme. For if *The Trial* rewrites the apocalyptic text of *Bleak House* it does so by refusing its solace and so intensifying the depiction of the demonic world. This is no less an example of radical typology than is Kafka's revision of the Judaic legacy itself. That is why we may place Kafka with Freud as a myth-maker of the modern era, conscious that myth-making is inseparable from mythic reading. Where Freud confronts us with an intolerable past, Kafka confronts us with an intolerable future. But again, as with Freud, Kafka seems to close off possibilities only to reopen them: his enigmatic vision demands that the reader, aware that she is in the presence of myth, must return again and again to the text in search of its elusive power. Kafka's very deconstruction of the principle of hope is itself apocalyptic: it unsettles, challenges and reorients the present.

THE SEARCH FOR THE SELF

Freud had numerous disciples, the most famous being Carl Jung (1875–1961). Jung broke with him in and around the time of

Totem and Taboo, disillusioned with his master's identification of the psyche with sexuality. Perhaps we might explain their differences more exactly by taking the Greek hero myth of Theseus' battle with the minotaur, and seeing how their interpretations might differ.

Theseus, the son of Aegeus, king of Attica, volunteers to become one of the victims provided as human food for the minotaur, a monster which is half-man and half-bull. Every year, due to a grievance held against Aegeus by Minos, king of Crete, seven young men and seven young women have to be shipped over to that island and forced to enter the labyrinth which was built for the creature by Daedalus the craftsman. There they will die. Theseus is determined to end this practice and, volunteering to lead the expedition, promises his father that when he returns to Athens he will indicate that he has succeeded in defeating the monster by displaying white sails; if not, he will display black. On arrival on Crete, he meets and seduces Ariadne, Minos' daughter and the minotaur's half-sister, and she offers to help him, on condition that he will marry her. After Theseus is shut up in the labyrinth, he does manage to slay the monster. He is only able to escape, however, with the aid of Ariadne, who provides him with a thread by which he finds his way out of the underground maze. On his way home, Theseus decides to abandon his new wife, and sails off without her when they break their journey at the island of Naxos. She curses him as he goes, but is soon rescued by the god Dionysus, who takes her as his mate. Meanwhile Theseus and his companions sail on, but so excited is he by his own triumph that he forgets to change the sails. When Aegeus, standing on a cliff, sees the black sails approaching from afar, he throws himself into the sea (thereafter known as the 'Aegean') and is drowned.

A Freudian reading of this myth would emphasise the repressed Oedipal desire of the hero, or ego, Theseus. Not intending to 'kill' his father, he unconsciously 'forgets' to change the sails, and so effectively provokes Aegeus to commit suicide. The myth, then, is about the inevitability of the son needing and wishing to replace the father. And sure enough, with Aegeus dead, Theseus does indeed assume the throne of Athens – his reign being suitably turbulent and his own end being violent.

A Jungian reading would focus not on the Oedipal conflict but on the task itself. Theseus, the young male hero, is only able to negotiate the depths of the labyrinth, representing the unconscious, by trusting to the help of Ariadne, representing female intuition. His subsequent abandonment of Ariadne would, then, symbolise the reassertion of aggressive, male rationality, for which a price must be paid, symbolised by the violent end of both father and son. In Jung's own terminology, which only partially derives from Freud's, we would say that the 'ego' (Theseus) is able to encounter and assimilate the power of the 'shadow' (minotaur) under the inspiration of the 'anima' (Ariadne). If, having done so, he chooses to ignore the further direction indicated by the 'anima', he will not be able to approach the wisdom of the 'self'.

These terms, which we will explain shortly, represent what Jung, and Eliade after him, calls 'archetypes'. Literally, an archetype is an original or founding image or figure. In *The Psychology of the Unconscious* (1913), later retitled *Symbols of Transformation*, Jung goes further: for him archetypes are permanent, eternal patterns of understanding. Though unrepresentable in themselves, they are made manifest as 'archetypal images'. These are universal motifs that come from the 'collective unconscious' and are the basic content of religions and mythologies. They emerge in individuals through dreams and visions. The 'collective unconscious' is inherited not acquired. It is true that Freud refers in *Totem and Taboo* to 'the heritage of emotion' and in *Moses and Monotheism* to 'the archaic heritage' (Freud 1985: 221, 343), but his point is that certain symbols evolved as a result of the historic (or, more accurately, pre-historic) trauma of the primal crime. For Jung, the symbols are simply there, buried and waiting in the universal psyche: 'There is no difference in principle between organic and psychic growth. As a plant produces its flower, so the psyche creates its symbols' (Jung 1990: 64). The task of life is to come to terms with the contents of the individual unconscious through relating them to those of the collective.

Moreover, where Freud is mainly interested in myths as the expression of sexual anxiety and conflict, Jung looks for signs of the impulse towards sacred meaning. Where Freud sees neurosis as the compulsion to remember, return and repeat, Jung sees neurosis as a sign that the soul yearns for something beyond physical or material satisfactions. Where Freud sees dream as a distorted fulfilment of a sexual wish, Jung sees dream as a natural expression of the psyche, by which it tries to heal itself. Thus, though it is Jung who speaks of 'archetypes', it is Freud who is the true 'archeologist' of the mind. Jung's interest is less in how the psyche evolved, and more in its spiritual goal or purpose. He offers, we might say, a 'teleology' of the spirit (Greek, *telos*, 'end'). Where Freud constantly looks back to childhood trauma, both in the individual and in the race, Jung looks forwards to mature adulthood. What is interesting for him is not how we learn to live, as sexual beings, but how we are going to face, as spiritual beings, our own deaths. He calls this process, this discovery of psychic harmony beyond the ego, 'individuation': the experience of the 'self' as the regulating centre of the psyche. Thus when Jung considers 'archetypes' he is looking for clues to the religious nature of humanity. Religion for him is the expression not of acquired guilt but of that urge which is natural to humans, to be at one with oneself and the cosmos. This urge is evident for him in all narratives, whether sacred or secular. It is just that one has to look harder for them in the latter.

In Jung's own mythic model, there are four main archetypes which tell us the story, as it were, of the psyche. Though collective, they have to be realised at the individual level. Firstly, there is the 'ego', the conscious mind; this is one's sense of purpose and identity. Secondly, there is the 'shadow', the unconscious aspect of the psyche which the ego tends to reject or ignore, usually symbolised in dreams by a figure of the same sex as the ego. The ego, if it is to develop, must face and assimilate the power of the shadow. Thirdly, there is the 'anima' (Latin, 'soul'), the unconscious, feminine side of a male personality; or the 'animus' (Latin, 'spirit'), the unconscious, male side of a woman's personality. In short, the one is the man's inner woman; the other is the woman's inner man. If these are positive images, they may inspire the ego to undertake the journey through and beyond the realm of the shadow. Fourthly, there is the 'self': the central archetype, that of the fulfilment of potential and the integration of personality. Frequently symbolised by a mandala or magic circle, it is the psychic totality towards which all life moves. Indeed, we may infer that the very journey from ego to self is circular, involving descent into the darkness of shadow and ascent towards the light of self. There is obviously a rough parallel with Frazer's cycle of the dying and reviving god, or even Eliade's eternal return, by which cosmos emerges from chaos; but here the ultimate model is psychological integration.

As we have seen, in the Theseus myth, the hero is the ego, the minotaur is the shadow and Ariadne is the anima. The self is not represented, which means that this is merely a hero myth and not a 'wisdom' myth. The latter, which is for Jung the most important kind, would seem to be roughly parallel to what Weston means by a 'Mystery' narrative. The paradox of Theseus is that his material success is really a kind of spiritual failure. For a model of attainment of the self we might perhaps turn to the myths of Jesus Christ and of Orpheus. In both cases material failure leads to spiritual success. Jesus is crucified as a common criminal, but is then resurrected as the Christ. Orpheus' story is less familiar, and may appear very different, but there is an underlying pattern in common. Orpheus, a musician and poet, allows his very concern for his wife Eurydice to prevent him bringing her back from the dead: forbidden to look back towards her on their way up from the underworld, he cannot help but do so in his anxiety for her safe release. But having lost his wife, and then having been dismembered by angry women for neglecting his arts in mourning, he becomes the object of an esoteric religious cult, his music and poetry symbolising cosmic harmony. Both Jesus Christ and Orpheus, then, may be taken to be embodiments of the self.

There is some difficulty in applying Jung's sequence of archetypes to literature, since very few texts represent the completed process. The nearest equivalent might be Dante's *Divine Comedy*, in which the poet/ego has to descend into the world of the shadow, or hell, where he meets many demonic doubles of himself, and even sees that greatest shadow of all, Satan. Then, guided by Beatrice, his anima, he is able to ascend to heaven and attain a total vision of the cosmos and of his place within it, thus acquiring the harmony of the self. It is especially significant that his journey takes place in a dream; we are to infer, in the Jungian perspective, that when he awakes and returns to temporal existence, he will have learnt how to balance the conscious and unconscious aspects of his psyche. Another, less obvious example might be *Faust*, Parts I and II (1808 and 1831), by Johann Wolfgang von Goethe. The protagonist is a middle-aged alchemist who sells his soul to Satan, in exchange for diabolical powers. Possessing these, and aided by Satan's servant Mephistopheles, he proceeds to seduce and abandon an innocent young woman, Margareta. Then, having gained the love of the legendary Helen of Troy, which ultimately proves insufficient, he achieves the full expression of his powers in, of all things, the project of reclaiming land from the sea. His material victory is complete, but the end of Part II shows him having to be redeemed by the intervention of Margareta and the healing powers of 'the eternal feminine'. Here, then, we have Faust as the ego, Mephistopheles as the shadow, Margareta as the positive anima, Helen of Troy as the negative anima, and the Mater

Gloriosa, or queen of Heaven, as the self. (Faust, it is implied, will take some time to attain true selfhood.)

Recognising the difference between Margareta and Helen is important, for we must not make the mistake of seeing Jung's archetypes as simple signposts on the route to spiritual realisation. They are supposed to indicate the complexity of the psyche. Thus the positive anima is not the same as the negative anima. By the same token, the negative anima must not be blandly subsumed within the shadow. Indeed, we must avoid the temptation to see all demonic figures as examples of the latter. The shadow is the dark side of the ego, and usually of the same sex: the demonic, murdering brother (Cain to Abel in the Book of Genesis, or Set to Osiris in the Egyptian myth of fertility), or else the alter ego (Enkidu the wild man to Gilgamesh the great king in the Babylonian epic *Gilgamesh*, or Mr Hyde to Dr Jekyll in Stevenson's novel). Though he may be monstrous, as is the minotaur, all monsters are not shadows. In the medieval romance of St George and the dragon, the dragon is the negative anima, the danger of regressing to the stupor of the maternal womb; George must overcome this danger if he is to save and marry the damsel, who is the positive anima of psychic development. The Bible is full of both negative and positive animas: for example, Eve and (as young maiden) Mary; Delilah and Ruth; the whore of Babylon and the bride of Jerusalem. It is easy to see how the Hollywood film industry constructs approximations of positive animas, such as Marilyn Monroe, but Jung would see these as inadequate models. Cinema is much more convincing when it comes to the negative anima: for example, the demonic female played by Sharon Stone in *Basic Instinct*; or the ubiquitous, creeping 'thing' which the character Ripley refers to as 'bitch' in the *Alien* trilogy. The latter is a particularly interesting example, for if the alien is of the same sex as the female protagonist, then it also constitutes Ripley's shadow. Either way, the film offers a fascinating twist to the usual pattern of the male warrior, such as Marduk or St George, fighting the female monster, such as Tiamat or the dragon. Less controversially, the nineteenth-century English novel seems particularly inclined to the figure of the animus. Again, we have negative and positive: Wickham and Darcy in Jane Austen's *Pride and Prejudice*, Casaubon and Ladislaw in George Eliot's *Middlemarch*. Or, particularly in the fiction of the Brontë sisters, we have the negative turning into the positive as a result of the dedication of the female protagonist: Heathcliff in *Wuthering Heights*, Rochester in *Jane Eyre*. As for the fourth main archetype: though it is rare to see the whole sequence of psychic growth depicted, we can find plenty of images of the self in fiction, film and song. Again, we have male and female aspects, which in effect are secondary, autonomous archetypes. There is the 'wise old man', such as Merlin in Arthurian romance, Gandalf in Tolkein's *The Lord of the Rings*, or Obi-Wan Kenobi in George Lucas's *Star Wars*. And there is the 'great mother', such as the fairy godmother in 'Cinderella', the Good Witch of the North in *The Wizard of Oz*, or 'Mother Mary' in the Beatles' 'Let It Be'.

Assessing Jung's contribution to mythography, we may make the following positive points. Firstly, he denies the Enlightenment faith in the power of reason, and trusts to the power of myth. Secondly, he demonstrates that the sacred may be manifest in the profane, and that this manifestation may take a variety of forms. We may even go so far as to say, with Edward Casey, that the psyche he discovers is 'at once prepersonal and pluripersonal (or more exactly, omnipersonal)': he stresses creativity and improvisation rather than stable identity (Barnaby and D'Acierno 1990: 322). He thus demonstrates that the mythic life is a matter of role-playing as much as authenticity: indeed, without 'image-ination', the willingness to live symbolically, there can be no 'individuation'. Thirdly, Jung does not, unlike many of those who borrow his terminology, such as Joseph Campbell, identify myth with mysticism as well as with mystery: he is not advocating 'absorption in the unconscious' but rather a condition of equilibrium: 'neither rejection of the unconscious nor surrender to it' (Segal 1987: 133). Indeed he argues against the merger of the ego in the self, a condition which he calls 'inflation' and which he sees as leading to a form of psychosis. In his *Archetypes and the Collective Unconscious* (1959) Jung states: 'the great psychic danger which is always connected with individuation . . . lies in the identification of ego-consciousness with the self. This produces an inflation which threatens consciousness with dissolution.' Quoting and commenting on this, Robert Segal remarks: 'The Jungian aim is no more to reject ego consciousness for the unconscious than, like the modern aim, to reject the unconscious for ego consciousness. The aim is, rather, to balance the two' (Jung 1992: 23).

Any dissatisfaction we feel with Jung's mythography may well focus on his concept of the archetype, which may be interpreted in two ways, realist and non-realist:

> There are no inborn ideas, but there are inborn possibilities of ideas that set bounds to even the boldest fantasy and keep our fantasy activity within certain categories: *a priori* ideas, as it were, the existence of which cannot be ascertained except from their effects.
>
> (Jung 1966: 81)

On the one hand, we could emphasise what we have emphasised above: the Jung of permanent possibility. On the other hand, we could emphasise a Jung who still clings to the universal and eternal forms of Plato. We might call this Jung a proponent of traditional realism, both psychological and metaphysical. Eric Gould calls him an 'essentialist' and a 'fundamentalist': whatever scope he seems to offer for the secular imagination, he will always insist that beyond it lies the indispensable source of all images, the truth which exceeds all narratives (Gould 1981: 15–16). The realm of the sacred ultimately transcends that of the profane, no matter that the former must find expression in the latter. Jung is, as it were, looking down from one to the other: he presumes the perspective of perfection. If Gould is right, then Jung is much less of a mythopoeic figure than is Freud. Indeed, we have only to remind ourselves of the distinction between the eternal archetype and the dialectic of type and anti-type to realise that Jung is above all an allegorist. He wants all myths to point towards his own model of harmony. As G.S. Kirk observes, Jung's ultimate aim is the 'stasis' of symbolism rather than the 'dynamism' of narrative (Kirk 1970: 278–80).

THE GRAMMAR OF THE MIND

Perhaps the most thorough-going search for stasis in the twentieth century has been the procedure known as 'structuralism'. Its most celebrated application to myth is that of the anthropologist Claude Lévi-Strauss. He may be aligned with Freud and Jung in so far as his subject is the workings of the human mind, and it might be worth making an initial, broad comparison. Thus Lévi-Strauss, sharing many of the assumptions of psychoanalysis, agrees with Freud that the meaning of myth is unconscious, and that human culture is always and everywhere characterised by the taboo against incest and patricide. But he rejects the biological model of instincts from which Freud starts. Again, we may say that both Jung and Lévi-Strauss take a synchronic and spatial view of myth rather than a diachronic and temporal view; and both are concerned with the collective psyche. But the former sees his archetypes as having an eternal quality beyond their various manifestations, while the latter insists that the units of myth, or 'mythemes', make sense only in relation to other units. This in itself, however, implies abstraction, for if the key to myth is language, with the mythemes functioning like phonemes or words, then for Lèvi-Strauss the key to both is grammar. In interpreting myth, we are not to attend to the single symbol but to the overall structure; not to what it may or may not mean to the individual, but to the communal logic which is implicit. Hence: 'myths get thought in man unbeknownst to him'; mythography is 'the quest for the invariant, or for the invariant among superficial differences' (Lévi-Strauss 1978: 3, 8). Thus in reading Lévi-Strauss we may have the curious impression of leaving behind other mythographers, all of whom may suddenly appear somewhat naive, while at the same time wondering if we have not been here before:

> To speak of rules and to speak of meaning is to speak of the same thing; and if we look at all the intellectual undertakings of mankind, as far as they have been recorded all over the world, the common denominator is always to introduce some kind of order. If this represents a basic need for order in the human mind and since, after all, the human mind is only part of the universe, the need probably exists because there is some order in the universe and the order is not a chaos.
>
> (Lévi-Strauss 1978: 12–13)

On the one hand, we are reminded of Eliot's 'mythical method' and so of a certain strain in modernism. On the other hand, we are reminded of the ambition of modernity, to abstract and rationalise everything. Either way, what is likely to suffer from this obsession with 'order' is the dynamism of the particular myth under consideration. Moreover, the claim to have inferred the absolute truth about the universe suggests that the mythic reading undertaken will be realist in principle rather than non-realist.

Lévi-Strauss's interpretation of the Oedipus myth has the advantage over Freud's that he does not confine himself to Sophocles' version. It has the disadvantage that he does not tell the whole story: the mythemes appear as if from nowhere in his own 'arrangement'. Hence the reader finds herself confronted by four columns of narrative items, respectively containing such cryptic and non-chronological information as: (1) 'Cadmos seeks his sister, ravished by Zeus' (Cadmos being the founder of Thebes); (2) 'Eteocles kills his brother Polynices' (both being sons of Oedipus fighting for the right to rule in his place); (3) 'Cadmos kills the dragon' (sent by Zeus to hinder his pursuit of himself and Europa); (4) 'Oedipus = *swollen-foot*?' (referring to his being tied down when abandoned as a baby). The key to these sets of mythemes is the opposition that Lévi-Strauss regards as the most fundamental of all, that of culture and nature. From this all others follow: order and chaos, life and death, self and other, eternity and time. It is the task of myth to articulate such contradictions, and so resolve them. Moreover, whatever the contradictions of the particular myth, the resolution achieved will be, in essence, that of culture and nature. The manifest concern may be familial affection, expressed in extreme form by incest (column 1), as opposed to familial aggression, expressed in extreme form by patricide or fratricide (column 2). On the other hand, it may be our attempt to sever contact with the earth from which we originated, as symbolised by killing monsters (column 3), as opposed to the fact that we cannot entirely leave our origins behind, as symbolised by lameness or difficulty in walking upright (column 4). But the latent concern will be the most fundamental of all: how the same relates to the other, how unity relates to division; in short, how culture relates to nature. As Lévi-Strauss puts it:

> the overrating of blood relations is to the underrating of blood relations as the attempt to escape autocthony [earthly origin] is to the impossibility to succeed in it. Although experience contradicts theory, social life validates cosmology by its similarity of structure. Hence cosmology is true.
>
> (Lévi-Strauss 1968: 216)

That is, culture (the familiar, or 'familial', world of columns 1 and 2, concerning our valuation of kinship) and nature (the unfamiliar world of columns 3 and 4, concerning our relation to the earth) have been mediated. Moreover, there has been a simultaneous resolution within culture: it is wrong to commit incest and patricide, and it is right to marry outside your clan. And that resolution involves a kind of compromise with nature: we admit that we originally sprang from earth, but reserve the right to go beyond it.

Though Lévi-Strauss is indebted to psychoanalysis, in that he assumes the above process of resolution to be unconscious and in that he takes the taboo against incest and patricide to be decisive, his reading of Oedipus is quite unlike that of Freud. Where Lévi-Strauss arrests the narrative in order to discover the logic, Freud produces his own narrative within which to situate the one he has received. Lévi-Strauss explains myth; Freud, where he manages to evade the legacy of the Enlightenment, explores and expands myth. The one is interested in abstraction, stasis and system; the other is interested in the dynamics of culture, understood as narrative. In short, unlike Freud at his most interesting, Lévi-Strauss is both a realist and an allegorist. His 'quest for the invariant', his obsession with 'rules', his insistence on 'order': these are indices of a mind which prefers *logos* to *mythos*, and (though without the Christian implication) the Word to words. For in his hands each myth turns out to be about the code of every myth, the metalanguage which informs and constrains all tellings of tales.

That said, structuralism has proved quite fruitful, in a simplified form, in the analysis of popular narrative forms. Its method of decoding has been applied with interesting results to the Western genre of film, a modern variation on hero myth, by Will Wright. He suggests that this genre is structured through certain basic oppositions, which are variants of the culture–nature division. It is through these that we initially situate all those opposites which motivate the plot, the most obvious being heroes and villains.

Wright distinguishes between the 'classic' or naive Western, such as *Dodge City* (1930), and the 'professional' or more sophisticated Western, such as *Butch Cassidy and the Sundance Kid* (1970). In the former, we know where we stand because we know where the hero stands: that is, with civilisation, society, the good; and against the wilderness, that which lies outside society, the bad. In the latter, while relying on the essential structure of opposition for our bearings, we are able to entertain the possibility that life may be more complicated. The hero here is more likely to be identified with the wilderness, and to be antagonistic to the society: hence we are no longer sure who is good and who is bad (G. Turner 1988: 88–9). It is important, of course, that the viewer is still relying on the essential structure of opposition, that between culture and nature, for her bearings. Without this paradigm, the film would not be able to explore variations of alignment or to mediate satisfactorily the contradictions of cultural experience itself, which is the focus of myth.

This kind of analysis works well on Westerns, which make a point of displaying their mythic structure. It is perhaps more difficult to read classic literary texts in terms of the nature–culture opposition. Here we do better if we remain alert to any suggestion at all of contradictions being mediated. Thus Austen's *Sense and Sensibility* obviously invites a structuralist reading: initially, there is too much 'sense' in Elinor Dashwood and too much 'sensibility' in her sister Marianne; the novel shows us that the human norm lies somewhere between. Another example might be Milton's *Paradise Lost*. On the one hand God foresees all events, including the fall from paradise; on the other hand Adam and Eve choose to commit sin quite freely. This epic poem might then be seen as a long and complex mediation, by which necessity and freedom turn out to be aspects of the same divine wisdom. Again, we might even see *Hamlet* as an extended enactment of the opposition between the contradictory impulses of the prince's most famous soliloquy: 'To be' and 'not to be'. The drama resolves these by letting Hamlet 'be' until the time comes 'not to be', when his father's death is avenged: an act which both negates and affirms his own identity. Here a certain strain is evident in the reading, and we might well conclude, after trying out a few examples, that there is a limited potential to such decoding: one cannot help but feel that, in pursuit of the grammar of the mind, one is leaving out almost everything that makes the interpretation of the particular text interesting. The richness of narrative is being reduced to the common denominator of universal 'order'.

Thus, despite the above evidence of a frutiful influence within cultural studies, we might want to agree with the anthropologist Clifford Geertz that the lasting impression of structuralist mythography is its abstraction and its essentialism. Geertz reflects that 'what Lévi-Strauss has made for himself is an infernal cultural machine. It annuls history, reduces sentiment to a shadow of intellect.' His 'search is not after all for men, whom he doesn't much care for, but for Man, with whom he is enthralled'. In short, his structuralism amounts to little more than 'hypermodern intellectualism' (Geertz 1993: 356–9). Geertz himself, by contrast, recognises the primacy of language without subscribing to a metalanguage. Indeed, his is an anthropology which constantly reflects on its own status as a linguistic construct. Inspired by the thought of Paul Ricoeur and Kenneth Burke, Geertz denies any claim to transcendent objectivity, and views his own interpretation as discourse and rhetoric (Geertz 1993: 19, 29). He knows, unlike Lévi-Strauss, that reading myth is also mythic reading.

Another anthropologist, Victor Turner, has sought to demonstrate the limits of the very principle of structure. If we think of it not simply as an abstract pattern but as a cultural assumption, we see how dangerous it may become. 'Structure' for Turner can all too often be a closed and static system, 'arid and mechanical'. Countering this there has to be what he calls 'communitas', a much more 'elusive' concept, but pragmatically important:

> All human societies implicitly refer to two contrasting social models. One . . . is of a society as a structure of jural, political

and economic positions, offices, statuses and roles, in which the individual is only ambiguously grasped behind the social persona. The other is of society as a communitas of concrete, idiosyncratic individuals who, though differing in physical and mental endowment, are nevertheless regarded as equal in terms of shared humanity.

(V. Turner 1974: 166)

Turner associates 'structure' with secular hierarchy and 'communitas' with any religious vision which offers a corrective to that order. He refers us to St Francis of Assisi who, taking a vow of marriage to 'Lady Poverty', rejected both the world of property and an all too worldly ecclesiastical establishment. Significantly, perhaps, he was a near-contemporary of Joachim, his followers, including Dante, tended also to be influenced by the abbot of Fiore.

'Communitas', moreover, being transitional, marginal, 'liminal', corresponds to that moment in what Arnold Van Gennep calls a 'rite of passage' when the initiate is placed outside society, on the 'threshold' (Latin, *limen*). The separation of the initiate is thought to coincide with the suspension of normal social rules, so that the 'post-liminal' phase of reintegration involves rebirth not only for the individual but also for the community. Thus, where 'structure' insists on identity and certainty, 'communitas' allows scope for difference and ambiguity, and so for potential (V. Turner 1974: 81–2). One cannot help but recall here Rickword's case for 'The Returning Hero', for the 'humorous' view of the universe which reinvigorates 'the social mind'. As for the early Rickword, so for Turner: far from being parasitic upon 'structure', or incidental to society, the 'liminality' of 'communitas' is essential to human development. Without such risk-takers as St Francis, the given hierarchy will tend to inertia, rigidifying injustice and inequality; and conversely, spontaneous spirituality has to have some order to test itself against, some threshold to cross. Thus we see that Turner's model is analogous not only to 'The Returning Hero' but also to

Ricoeur's 'dialectic of ideology and utopia' and to Burke's 'comic corrective'. It assumes myth to be active within history.

Another thinker who is concerned with collective logic yet who cannot be contained by the terms of structuralist mythography is the literary theorist René Girard. An opponent of Freud (and with him, Frazer) as much as of Lévi-Strauss, he yet begins from both their premisses. With Freud, he believes that human culture has its roots in violence; with Lévi-Strauss, he believes that myth is traditionally about 'order'. But he goes beyond both, in a direction that aligns him with Turner, Ricoeur and Burke. His decisive break with Freud is over the Oedipus complex, which in *Violence and the Sacred* he rejects in favour of a theory of 'mimetic desire'. He argues that violence threatens wherever one person wants to imitate another person, to have what they have or to be what they are, but is prevented from doing so by lack of resources or status. This desire to imitate the chosen model, if universally expressed, leads to a chronic and 'impure' violence. In order to purge itself of this disease, society decides on an act of abrupt and 'pure' violence. It selects at random a victim, a 'scapegoat', and kills him, thus directing the collective violence away from the group (Girard 1977: 39–51). Unlike Frazer's model, in which a particular man must be murdered because he is thought to represent the god, for Girard the choice of victim is arbitrary; it is only after the event that the scapegoat is deified. Unlike Freud's model, it is not the son killing the father that matters (except in so far as he wishes to 'imitate' him, and marry the mother), but society preventing its own self-destruction. Hence Girard reads Sophocles' *Oedipus Rex* as concerning the 'sacrificial crisis': Oedipus is the 'surrogate victim' who is destroyed by his society, not because he is supposed to have done anything wrong, but because it is contriving to hide from itself the real causes of its internal crisis: it needs a scapegoat (Girard 1979: 84–5). Girard's account here owes much to Burke's suggestion that 'perfectionism' taken to the extreme involves systematic aggression.

Thus far, Lévi-Strauss might agree with Girard: myth is about the threat of 'disorder' and the need for 'order'. But the latter parts company with structuralism when, in *The Scapegoat* (1986) and *Things Hidden since the Foundation of the World* (1987), he argues that myths need to be questioned as texts which justify persecution. Against the sacrificial logic of myth, which for Girard always takes the side of victors against victims, he proposes the anti-sacrificial vision of scripture. The God we discover in the Bible is the God of the victims. In particular, the example and parables of Jesus Christ repudiate the sacralisation of violence. In effect, they declare an end to the scapegoat mechanism, the crucifixion being the sacrifice of an entirely innocent victim whose very aim is the end of all sacrifices. The message we receive from the Gospels is that of love, forgiveness and non-violence. With Victor Turner, Girard believes this kind of imaginative thinking involves a crossing of thresholds, a leap into uncertainty. The irony is, of course, that Christianity itself soon became, and for many remains, a sacrificial religion (as noted by Freud in *Moses and Monotheism*). It has always been ready to create scapegoats and to relish victimage (to use Kenneth Burke's term). Thus, as might be expected, T.S. Eliot in his play *Murder in the Cathedral* (1935) finds it entirely appropriate to fuse Frazerian mythography and Christian doctrine in his celebration of the martyrdom of Thomas Becket. He accepts, that is, the very logic which Girard is repudiating. There can be little doubt that the author concurs with the chorus when, after the event, it thanks God for the 'blood of Thy martyrs and saints' which shall 'enrich the earth' (Eliot 1961: 71). The protagonist, too, confirming the chorus's understanding, speaks very much like the Eliot we already know, taking the 'sign of the Church' to be the 'sign of blood': 'His blood given to buy my life' and 'My blood given to pay for His death' (Eliot 1961: 60–1). This kind of Christianity stands in relation to Girard's as type to anti-type. Its sacralisation of violence is mythic, if we agree with the speaker in Geoffrey Hill's poem 'Genesis': 'There is no bloodless myth will hold' (Hill 1985: 16). But perhaps, even given Girard's view that Christianity deconstructs the logic of sacrifice, the faith he espouses may be seen as more than demythologization. For his purpose is not to replace *mythos* with *logos*, if by the latter we mean hierarchical doctrine. Rather, he is correcting one sort of story by means of another. Christianity is no less a myth than the story of the scapegoat which it rewrites. Thus Girard may be said to be a demythologizer in that he repudiates the literalism evident in the relish for 'blood' in the lines just quoted. At the same time, Girard may be said to be a remythologizer in that he endorses the symbolic potential of Christian narrative. Hence he might be aligned with Paul Ricoeur. It is Ricoeur, we recall, who speaks of myth as a 'disclosure' of 'possible worlds'. For him the Gospel story of the resurrection offers 'freedom in the light of hope': it displays a 'logic of surplus and excess' and 'an *economy of superabundance*' (Ricoeur 1974: 410). As such, *pace* Bultmann, it cannot be demythologized, any more than the profane imagination can cease producing stories of the sacred. In the next chapter we will consider how that imagination has become more important than ever in the present era.

6

HISTORY

CRITICISM AS ROMANCE

The year 1957 saw the publication of two books which have remained deeply influential: *Mythologies* by Roland Barthes (1915 –80) and *Anatomy of Criticism* by Northrop Frye (1912–91). We will consider Barthes's book first, but must begin by recognising that, though its title seems the more relevant to our discussion, the work itself is less about mythology than about ideology, and that in the pejorative sense of mystification. Or, to be more accurate, for Barthes the two terms are interchangeable. Thus there is a 'mythology of wine', predicated on certain assumptions about health and social behaviour, which attributes magical properties to the French national drink: 'it is above all a converting substance, capable of reversing situations and states, and of extracting from objects their opposites – for instance, making a weak man strong or a silent one talkative'. But it also serves to distract consumers from the fact that the production of wine is 'deeply involved in French capitalism'. It is a drink which 'cannot be an unalloyedly blissful substance, except if we wrongly forget that it is also the product of an expropriation' (Barthes 1973: 61). Other 'myths' considered include a black soldier saluting the French flag on a magazine cover, Roman haircuts in Hollywood films, the face of Greta Garbo, steak and chips, striptease, the Citroen car, and a wrestling match.

Though we call this kind of analysis structuralist, we should distinguish it from the decoding which we have already encountered. For one thing, the very material studied is different. Lévi-Strauss is concerned with archaic or primitive narratives which reveal something of the workings of a universal human mind. Barthes is concerned with the peculiar workings of contemporary communications and media. Also, they differ as to intentions and interests. Lévi-Strauss sets out to demonstrate that culture and nature are mediated through the logic or grammar of the myth, and concludes that this is a necessary activity of the human mind. Barthes sets out to demonstrate that culture and nature are in effect identified, and concludes that this is a sinister deception. In more detail, we may say of Barthes that he exposes 'mythology' as the systematic presentation of bourgeois thinking as if it were the only possible way of thinking: 'what goes without saying'. Thus 'myth' is 'depoliticized speech' which represses the 'contingent, historical, in one word: *fabricated*' quality of capitalism (Barthes 1973: 143). Bourgeois ideology pretends that the cultural construction is a natural phenomenon.

This kind of analysis is necessary and it is impressive; but as *Mythologies* does not offer anything more positive, it has to be seen as a variation on demythologization, propounding its own myth of mythlessnesss. Barthes is implicitly claiming to be able to demystify the forces which hold others in thrall and so, presumably, transcend them. Unlike Bultmann, however, he does not need to locate and then set aside any narrative, since nearly all his subjects are non-narrative images or concepts. So it is not that *mythos* is being replaced by *logos*; rather, it is assumed to be a kind of false *logos* in the first place. Moreover, as each reading only repeats the same point, that beneath the apparently natural there lies the cultural, we might call Barthes's methodology a kind of political allegory. That said, the notion of the denial of history is an interesting one, and we will return to it later.

Those interested in discovering another Barthes, much more concerned with exploration than explanation, might consult the selection of essays written in the 1960s and early 1970s, *Image–Music–Text*. Though his 'Introduction to the Structural Study of Narratives' (1966) turns out to be little more attentive to story as story than is Lévi-Strauss's exposition of Oedipus, 'The Struggle with the Angel' (1971) offers some strikingly new insights. This analysis of Genesis 32: 22–32 relates the encounter between Jacob, the figure chosen by God to be the ancestor of the people of Israel, and an unidentified 'man' or angel, to the structure of folk tale. Ostensibly it is an application of the categories expounded by the Russian formalist critic Vladimir Propp in his *Morphology of the Folktale* (1928), a proto-structuralist work which treats popular narratives as rigidly rule-governed. But Barthes goes much further, trying to account for the strangeness of the episode. According to Propp's scheme, if this were a standard folk tale concerning 'the Quest', we would expect to distinguish between 'the Originator of the Quest', 'the Hero' who is on the quest, and 'the Opponent'. The crucial factor for Barthes is that in Genesis 32 the first and last of these are revealed to be one and the same. It is God who sends Jacob on his quest; it is God who, in the form of the 'man', wrestles with him at the fords of the Jabbok river, apparently seeking to destroy him. Barthes argues that the reason for this breach of the 'rules' is theological: the affirmation of monotheism. The God of the Israelites has to be thought of as so powerful that there could be no independent force strong enough to hinder one of his chosen servants. Hence the story is only allowed to be told so long as it does not offend against the hard-won doctrine of one almighty God. This in effect means that, though it is undoubtedly derived from non-Biblical sources, it has to be retold in such a way that it overrides the 'rules' of folk tale or legend. Thus Barthes's theological insight turns out to be a literary one. To quote John Barton's succinct summary of a complicated argument:

> Genesis 32 is able to have the effect it obviously does have on most readers only because it *first* constrains us to read it as if it were a normal folk-tale, and *then* turns the tables on us by illicitly exploiting the conventions of such tales. The result is a surrealistic sense of disorientation. A parallel from modern literature would be a detective novel where the detective himself turned out to be the murderer . . . . Consider [also], for example, the Middle English poem *Sir Gawain and the Green Knight*, where in the moment of disclosure we (and Gawain) learn that Sir Bertilak, his host, and the Green Knight, his adversary, are one and the same. The reader is likely to experience just the same shudder as in Genesis 32, and for the same reason: confusion of roles undermines our confidence that we know what we are reading.
>
> (Barton 1984: 118–19)

Thus Barthes has done more than explain the grammar or structure underlying the narrative expression: he has treated the particular story as an intervention in an inherited discourse. In short, he has stressed that sense of potential which we have associated with radical typology rather than with allegory. His closing comments are, then, particularly significant. He suggests that we pursue the 'dissemination' of the text, 'not its truth'. For the 'problem' Barthes takes to be crucial is 'exactly not to manage to reduce the Text to a signified, whatever it may be (historical, economic, folkloristic or kerygmatic), but to hold its *significance* fully open' (Barthes 1981: 141).

It is the Barthes of 'The Struggle with the Angel', not of *Mythologies*, who has the more affinities with Northrop Frye. But before considering the *Anatomy* as a genuinely mythopoeic work, we should acknowledge that, at first glance, it does look very much like a standard exposition of structuralist principles. Indeed, Frye states explicitly in his introduction that he intends to assert the 'science' of literary criticism and to counter 'appreciation', 'impressionism' and 'naive induction' (Frye 1971: 7, 15). It is written on the assumption that criticism can be scientific precisely because literature itself is 'not a piled aggregate of "works", but an order of words' (Frye 1971: 17). Value-judgements of individual texts are discounted in favour of 'the systematic study of the formal causes of art' (Frye 1971: 29). The form which is the 'cause' of the art of literature is myth: the 'modes' of literary narrative work according to the logic of 'displacement', which is the 'adaptation of myth . . . to canons of morality or plausibility' (Frye 1971: 365). The more literature distances itself from myth, moving from 'romance' through the 'mimetic' modes, the more 'real' it appears; though, as Frye indicates, this appearance is deceptive, as is evident once we reach the self-conscious exposure of device favoured by 'irony'.

Frye defines a narrative mode as a 'conventional power of action assumed about the chief characters in fictional literature', adding that they 'tend to succeed one another in a historical sequence' (Frye 1971: 366). He classifies them according to Aristotle's distinction between narratives in which 'the hero's power of action' is 'greater than ours, less, or roughly the same'. Extending three categories to five we get the following scheme:

1   If superior in *kind* both to other men and to the environment of other men, the hero is a divine being, and the story about him will be a *myth* in the common sense of a story about a god. Such stories have an important place in literature, but are as a rule found outside the normal literary categories.

2   If superior in *degree* to other men and to his environment, the hero is the typical hero of *romance*, whose actions are marvellous but who is himself identified as a human being. The

hero of romance moves in a world in which the ordinary laws of nature are slightly suspended: prodigies of courage and endurance, unnatural to us, are natural to him, and enchanted weapons, talking animals, terrifying ogres and witches, and talismans of miraculous power violate no rule of probability once the postulates of romance have been established . . . .

3 If superior in degree to other men but not to his natural environment, the hero is a leader. He has authority, passions, and powers of expression far greater than ours, but what he does is subject both to social criticism and to the order of nature. This is the hero of the *high mimetic* mode . . . .

4 If superior neither to other men nor to his environment, the hero is one of us: we respond to a sense of his common humanity, and demand from the poet the same canons of probability that we find in our own experience. This gives us the hero of the *low mimetic* mode . . . .

5 If inferior in power or intelligence to ourselves, so that we have the sense of looking down on a scene of bondage, frustration or absurdity, the hero belongs to the *ironic* mode. This is still true when the reader feels that he is or might be in the same situation, as the situation is being judged by the norms of a greater freedom.

(Frye 1971: 33–4)

Paradoxically, it is his initial simplification of paradigms, involving the characterisation of 'myth' as a narrative about a god, which allows Frye to offer his sophisticated account of the modes. This in turn allows him to accommodate all possible literary genres. 'Romance' covers, for example, legend and folk tale. The two 'mimetic' modes cover what is usually referred to as literary realism, but Frye makes it clear that, where we may think we are witnessing the representation of reality, we are actually enjoying works as conventional and stylised as those of myth or romance. Thus the 'high mimetic' covers, for example, epic and tragedy, which are, traditionally, highly structured works. The 'low mimetic' covers, for example, comedy, a term which in turn covers the eighteenth- and nineteenth-century novel: what is at work is 'the Cinderella archetype', which Frye describes as 'the incorporation of an individual very like the reader into the society aspired to by both, a society ushered in with a happy rustle of bridal gowns and banknotes' (Frye 1971: 44). That leaves only the 'ironic', which covers, for example, modernist poetry and fiction, satirical fantasy and the theatre of the absurd. This final mode, irony, frequently offers a disturbing parody of romance, as with the abortive quests of *Heart of Darkness* and *The Trial*: thus any illusion of realism we may have had in our experience of the 'mimetic' modes is dispelled.

The system is not completely watertight, however, as the awkward category of epic will indicate. Frye's inclusion of epic along with tragedy in the 'high mimetic' creates some confusion, because the main examples of the genre suggest it is closer to myth, or at least the paradigm of hero myth, than is romance. Thus the protagonist of the Babylonian *Gilgamesh*, though not a god, is semi-divine; though mortal, he is able to undertake the most marvellous adventures, akin to those of Perseus and Theseus. Frye, having defined myth as a narrative about a god, would have no choice but to place *Gilgamesh* in the sphere of literature. But there still remains the question of its proximity to myth. Frank McConnell, contradicting Frye, thinks it more logical to place epic above romance, the hero of the former usually being a king with divine authority and the hero of the latter usually being a knight or the equivalent (McConnell 1979: 3–20). In order to justify Frye's categorisation, one would have to translate 'epic' as 'secondary' or 'literary epic' (Jenkyns 1992: 53–6). This might be exemplified by Milton's *Paradise Lost*: though the heroism belongs to the son of God, who offers to counteract Satan and undo the results of the fall of Adam and Eve, it is they who are the actual protagonists, strictly speaking. Moreover, their narrative is the occasion of too many elaborate speculations (about predestination and free will, for example) to retain the impact of 'primary' epic.

Another problem with Frye's scheme is that while it seems to offer an insight into literary history, with the five modes following one another chronologically, this sequence runs the risk of abstraction. Thus, though it is broadly true that in English culture romance precedes realism, we might be tempted to infer from the opening paragraphs of the *Anatomy* that this process is universal and inevitable. But of course other cultures form their own histories; and romance can appear after realism, as it has done even in twentieth-century England, thanks to Tolkien, Lewis and others. In fact, Frye goes to some trouble later in his book to deny these implications, and to insist on the flexibility of his model. But certainly he frequently had to face the charge of being more synchronic than diachronic, and of being insensitive to particular cultures other than the Anglo-American. However, this charge may miss the point of his enterprise, which Paul Ricoeur describes as a celebration of an endlessly 'productive imagination' (Ricoeur 1991: 244).

Thus, used with discretion and flexibility, Frye's sequence can be at least as illuminating about literature as structuralism is about myth. It allows us to situate texts as cultural constructs belonging to an 'order of words' rather than encountering them as isolated and spontaneous phenomena which seem to have nothing in common. (In this sense the *Anatomy* owes something also to 'Tradition and the Individual Talent', though as we shall see, Frye has a very different idea from Eliot of what a 'mythical method' involves.) Thus if one knows a particular work is low mimetic, one knows not to have expectations of it that are more appropriate to romance: though both modes are 'displacements' from myth, the latter will be less 'plausible' than the former.

We might illustrate the four literary narrative types as follows, by listing some of their more famous protagonists. In romance we find: Robin Hood; Perceval; Chaucer's Aurelius ('The Franklin's

Tale'); Spenser's Red Cross Knight; Tarzan; Batman and Superman; Obi-Wan Kenobi and Luke Skywalker (*Star Wars*). In the high mimetic we find: Shakespeare's King Lear, Antony and Cleopatra, Othello and Hamlet; Milton's Adam and Eve. In the low mimetic we find: Shakespeare's Beatrice (*Much Ado about Nothing*) and Viola (*Twelfth Night*); Jane Austen's Fanny Price (*Mansfield Park*); Dickens's Pip (*Great Expectations*). In the ironic we find: Hardy's Tess; Kafka's Gregor Samsa ('Metamorphosis') and Joseph K; the inhabitants of Eliot's *Waste Land*; Orwell's Winston Smith (*Nineteen Eighty-Four*); Beckett's Vladimir and Estragon (*Waiting for Godot*).

So far we have a dispassionate account of a literary 'system', an 'order of words', which Lévi-Strauss might approve. But the *Anatomy* is much more than a demonstration of structure. For once Frye has listed his modes, and we have supplemented the catalogue with named characters and texts, we still have only begun. Here the difference from the Barthes of *Mythologies* needs stressing. Barthes equates myth with ideology: it confirms the status quo. Frye's model has utopian implications. For the sequence of modes is not meant to be an arid classification of forms, but is meant to demonstrate what Paul Ricoeur calls 'narrative understanding'. Frye is offering his own reading of myth, which he sees 'displaced' through the four modes of literature, as a mythic reading. With Blake, he is chiefly interested in myth as mythopoeia; and like him, he has his own story to recount. Unlike the early Barthes, who sees myth as culture disguised as nature, Frye wants to tell us about the transformation of nature into culture.

There are two paradigms implicit in this story of Frye's: the deliverance myth, as given in the Bible; and fertility myth, as given in *The Golden Bough*. The clue to both of these allusions comes at the end of the first of the four essays which comprise the *Anatomy*, in the following unassuming digression, which concerns the way literature not only has myth as its origin, even where it may seem to be concerned with 'verisimilitude', or semblance of actuality, but also as its destiny:

> Reading forward in history, therefore, we may think of our romantic, high mimetic and low mimetic modes as a series of *displaced* myths, *mythoi* or plot-formulas progressively moving over towards the opposite pole of verisimilitude, and then, with irony, beginning to move back.

(Frye 1971: 51–2)

That is, with the final narrative mode we are forcibly reminded that the first and founding mode, namely myth itself, has been ever-present beneath the apparent realism of literature, and we witness the reaffirmation of its 'formal cause'. Just as literature descends from myth, through romance downwards, so does irony return to myth. Again, as above, we can easily supply our own examples. Indeed, we know the following texts well: *The Waste Land, Ulysses, Finnegans Wake*, 'The End', *Dispatches* and *Apocalypse Now*. We have even encountered a manifesto of ironic mythopoeia, in the form of Edgell Rickword's essay, 'The Returning Hero'. Again, we know that Burke regards 'irony' as a dialectical force which, though it may appear merely disruptive and even destructive, is the necessary condition for the 'comic corrective' of 'perspective by incongruity'.

If we accept the principle of the return of irony to myth, then the pattern may be regarded as cyclical, as with Frazer's fertility myth. Significantly, the two central literary modes, the high and low mimetic, are most clearly represented by the genres of tragedy and comedy respectively. In one the hero falls from high to low, from life to death: for example, King Lear, Antony or Othello. In the other the hero rises like Cinderella from low to high, from a kind of death-in-life of obscurity and confusion, to a new way of life: for example, Viola, Fanny Price or Pip. This pattern of renewal, expanded, forms the cyclical movement of the four literary modes. Thus Frye's 'order of words' is reminiscent of the story of the dying god and the reviving god, representative as they are of the seasonal round. Thus the four *mythoi* are analogous to the four seasons: romance is the *mythos* of summer, the high mimetic (represented by tragedy) is that of autumn, irony of winter, and the low mimetic (represented by comedy) of spring. But at the same time, the cycle is contained by a larger pattern still, that implicit in 'the Great Code' itself. This is a design both cosmic and historical, concerning a heaven above and a hell below, and a creation at the beginning of time and a new creation at the end. Frye indicates this vast, inclusive framework by two kinds of symbolism: 'apocalyptic' and 'demonic'. These are the ultimate terms of the myth which contains, informs and moves literary expression. Their dialectic encompasses the cycle just outlined. Frye's *Anatomy*, his own mythic reading of literature, is an attempt to affirm the 'apocalyptic' vision as the permanent possibility which inspires the secular imagination. Thus by 'apocalyptic' he means, not the literal expectation of catastrophe, nor even a religious doctrine, but the imaginative anticipation of the not yet. It is the form which reality assumes under the aspect of 'desire', defined in its broadest sense as the wish for more abundant life. Here we encounter images such as the paradisal garden, the tree of life, the highway, the heavenly city, and the beatific lamb. To make sense, however, it must be balanced by a vision of the world which desire rejects: the 'demonic'. Here we encounter images such as the wilderness or the sinister forest, the tree of death, the labyrinth, the city of destruction and the serpent or dragon (Frye 1971: 141–50).

It will be clear by now that Frye is telling a story which implies a cosmology. It is the traditional Christian one: 'a heaven above, a hell beneath, and a cyclical . . . order of nature in between' (Frye 1971: 161). But he is reading it literarily not literally. Like literature itself, it is for him a vast, imaginative construct, not a representation of reality. Thus he gives special status to the first of the four literary modes, romance: with its sense of the marvellous, and its quest structure, it represents the power of the human mind to construct a cosmos according to the imperatives of desire. Indeed, he makes this one literary genre the subject of an entire book: *The Secular Scripture* (1976). In the *Anatomy* he tries to convey its significance as follows:

> The central form of quest-romance is the dragon-killing theme exemplified by the stories of St George and Perseus . . . . A land ruled by a helpless old king is laid waste by a sea-monster, to whom one young person after another is offered to be devoured, until the lot falls on the king's daughter: at that point, the hero arrives, kills the dragon, marries the daughter, and succeeds to the kingdom.
>
> (Frye 1971: 189)

The same pattern is evident in the last book of the Bible, which is the basis for 'an elaborate dragon-killing metaphor in Christian symbolism'. Drawing on suggestions in earlier books, that there is a sea-monster named the leviathan which is 'the enemy of the Messiah, and whom the Messiah is destined to kill in the "day of the lord"', the author of Revelation identifies the leviathan, Satan and the serpent of Eden. That is, 'the hero is Christ (often represented in art standing on a prostrate monster), the dragon Satan, the impotent old king Adam, whose son Christ becomes, and the rescued bride the Church' (Frye 1971: 189). Thus the secular romance, with its roots in the fertility cycle, and the sacred vision, with its dialectic of the apocalyptic and demonic, turn out to be complementary not contradictory. They both bear witness to the persistence and power of mythopoeia.

Frye pushes the possibilities of romance as far as he can by taking it to be a grand narrative in its own right. It is worth quoting his argument at length, as it incorporates many of the themes and motifs which we have encountered already:

The leviathan is usually a sea-monster, which means metaphorically that he *is* the sea, and the prophecy that the Lord will hook and land the leviathan in Ezekiel is identical with the prophecy in Revelation that there shall be no more sea. As denizens of his belly, therefore, we are also metaphorically under water. Hence the importance of fishing in the Gospels, the apostles being 'fishers of men' who cast their nets into the sea of this world. Hence, too, the later development, referred to in *The Waste Land*, of Adam or the impotent king as an ineffectual 'fisher king'. In the same poem the appropriate link is also made with Prospero's rescuing of a society out of the sea in *The Tempest* . . . . The insistence on Christ's ability to command the sea belongs to the same aspect of symbolism. And as the leviathan, in his aspect as the fallen world, contains all forms of life imprisoned within himself, so as the sea he contains the imprisoned life-giving rain waters whose coming marks the spring. The monstrous animal who swallows all the water in the world and is then teased or tricked or forced into disgorging it is a favorite of folk tales, and a Mesopotamian version lies close behind the story of Creation in Genesis . . . .

Lastly, if the leviathan is death, and the hero has to enter the body of death, the hero has to die, and if his quest is completed the final stage of it is, cyclically, rebirth, and, dialectically, resurrection. In the St George plays the hero dies in his dragon-fight and is brought to life by a doctor, and the same symbolism runs through all the dying-god myths.

(Frye 1971: 191–2)

On this evidence Frye infers that there are 'four aspects to the quest-myth', which may be related to the four literary modes themselves:

First, the *agon* or conflict itself. Second, the *pathos* or death, often the mutual death of hero and monster. Third, the disappearance of the hero, a theme which often takes the form of *sparagmos* or tearing to pieces. Sometimes the hero's body is divided among his followers, as in Eucharist symbolism: sometimes it is distributed around the natural world, as in the stories of Orpheus and more especially Osiris. Fourth, the reappearance and recognition of the hero, where sacramental Christianity follows the metaphorical logic: those who in the fallen world have partaken of their redeemer's divided body are united with his risen body.

The four *mythoi* that we are dealing with, comedy, romance, tragedy, and irony, may now be seen as four aspects of a central unifying myth. *Agon* or conflict is the basis or archetypal theme of romance, the radical of romance being a sequence of marvellous adventures. *Pathos* or catastrophe, whether in triumph or in defeat, is the archetypal theme of tragedy. *Sparagmos*, or the sense that heroism and effective action are absent, disorganized or foredoomed to defeat, and that confusion and anarchy reign over the world, is the archetypal theme of irony and satire. *Anagnorisis*, or recognition of a newborn society rising in triumph around a still somewhat mysterious hero and his bride, is the archetypal theme of comedy.

(Frye 1971: 192)

Hence history itself may be read in terms of this 'secular scripture'. Like the founding literary mode of romance, it may be taken to imply a narrative vision of desire frustrated and fulfilled. Frye being one of the 'Odyssey critics' rather than the 'Iliad critics' (Frye 1965: 1), he is more interested in the *agon* which leads to *anagnorisis* than in the *pathos* that deepens into *sparagmos*. For him, history is mythic in that it offers scope for comic affirmation of the human quest.

The use of the word 'archetypal' may suggest an affinity with Jung. But it must be remembered that Jung identifed his archetypes with a fixed, eternal world rather than a dynamic, historical one. Frye stresses the latter, even in the modest definition of 'archetype' given in the glossary to the *Anatomy*: 'A symbol, usually an image, which recurs often enough in literature to be recognisable as an element of one's literary experience as a whole' (Frye 1971: 365). What literary experience tells Frye, and what the above theoretical narrative tells us, is not that the 'secular scripture' of romance reflects an existing cosmos but that it creates it. It does so through the 'order of words'. Symbols and narrative patterns recur, and the more one recognises them, according to Frye, the more one is able to infer a vast quest-myth at work. The quest is for totality, for completeness, for perfection. That will never be achieved, but it is the task of the critic to maintain a sense of permanent possibility. For the critic too is engaged in a quest, and criticism is a kind of romance.

The paradox of Frye's position, as a Christian critic, is that in dignifying the secular imagination with the word 'scripture', he has to resist the claims of religion, at least in their fundamentalist form. For nothing is so antipathetic to his notion of permanent possibility as a literal reading of the Bible. Culture, which comprises myth and literature, is not to be identified with religion, if the latter is merely a matter of dogmatic assertion:

> Culture interposes, between the ordinary and the religious life, a total vision of possibilities, and insists on its totality – for whatever is excluded from culture by religion or state will get its revenge somehow. Thus culture's essential service to a religion is to destroy intellectual idolatory, the recurrent tendency in religion to replace the object of its worship with its present understanding and forms of approach to that object. Just as no argument in favor of a religious or political doctrine is of any value unless it is an intellectually honest argument, and so guarantees the autonomy of logic, so no religious or political myth is either valuable or valid unless it assumes the autonomy

of culture, which may be provisionally defined as the total body
of imaginative hypothesis in a society and its tradition.

(Frye 1971: 127)

One could not get a more clear reversal of Barthes's position in
Mythologies: where Barthes stresses the duplicitous and conspira-
torial aspects of bourgeois culture, binding us to the status quo,
Frye sees the culture of any age as carrying within it the potential
for freedom. Again, contrasting Frye with Eliot, we may observe
that the sequence of modes recalls the 'ideal order', but the
proponent of the latter finally decided to subordinate cultural
tradition to religious orthodoxy. Moreover, as Frye himself points
out in his study of the poet, Eliot's own view of history was deeply
conservative and pessimistic (Frye 1981: 7). It may have been a
myth, but it was certainly not a quest.

Thus the Bible in the *Anatomy* serves a similar function to
that of *The Golden Bough*. It provides food for the imagination.
Of Frazer's massive mythographic work he remarks that it is, 'as
literary criticism, an essay on the ritual content of naive drama':
that is, 'it reconstructs an archetypal ritual from which the structural and generic principles of drama may be logically derived'.
Thus: 'it does not matter two pins to the critic whether this ritual
ever had any *historical* existence or not' (Frye 1978: 125). Frye's
Frazer is a non-realist Frazer. As to the Bible: Frye devotes two
books to its formal analysis, *The Great Code* (1982) and *Words
with Power* (1990), and in the first of these gives an extremely
full account of scriptural typology (Frye 1982: 105–38). But it
becomes clear long before completing our reading of the first
volume that he is treating 'the Great Code' in a manner similar to
Blake's: not as a doctrinal constraint but as an imaginative agenda.
Thus, commenting on the Biblical creation myth as an anti-type
to existing ancient near eastern narratives, he suggests that 'we
take the Bible as a key to mythology, instead of taking mythology
in general as a key to the Bible' (Frye 1982: 92). An orthodox

Christian could not make such a suggestion. Again, thinking no doubt of Dante's own mythopoeic work, he has no qualms about using the Bible as an illustration of a secular narrative form, 'the U-shaped pattern' which is 'the standard shape of comedy':

> The entire Bible, viewed as a 'divine comedy', is contained within a U-shaped story of this sort, one in which each man . . . loses the tree and water of life at the beginning of Genesis and gets them back at the end of Revelation. In between, the story of Israel is told as a series of declines into the power of heathen kingdoms, Egypt, Philistia, Babylon, Syria, Rome, each followed by a brief moment of relative independence. The same U-narrative is found outside the historical sections also, in the account of Job and in Jesus' parable of the prodigal son.
>
> (Frye 1982: 169)

Though the emphasis here is on comedy rather than romance, Frye's point is that both sacred and secular scripture, perceived as a 'total vision of possibilities', or 'total body of imaginative hypothesis', are narrative projections. Neither flatly linear nor deterministically cyclical, they are best seen as negotiating 'the shape of history' and as working within the tension between 'temporal movement' and 'revelation' (Frye 1982: 198). The 'order of words' may imply the one 'Word', but what the Bible, mythology, literature and criticism all indicate to Frye is that travelling hopefully towards it may be as good as having arrived.

A SINGLE STORY?

> The greatness of Frye, and the radical difference between his work and that of the great bulk of garden-variety myth criticism, lies in his willingness to raise the issue of community and to draw basic, essentially social, interpretive consequences from the nature of religion as collective representation . . . .The

religious figures then become the symbolic space in which the collectivity thinks itself and celebrates its own unity; so that it does not seem a very difficult next step, if, with Frye, we see literature as a weaker form of myth or a later stage of ritual, to conclude that in that sense all literature, no matter how weakly, must be informed by what we have called a political unconscious, that all literature must be read as a symbolic meditation on the destiny of community.

(Jameson 1981: 69–70)

The writer of this commendation of Frye is a Marxist literary critic. In many respects Fredric Jameson's *The Political Unconscious* is a political revision of the *Anatomy*. Certainly, it owes far more to Frye's visionary criticism than it does to the 'scientific' or 'structural' Marxism of the late Louis Althusser. We might almost say that Frye offers Jameson his means of countering Althusser's challenge. That challenge is, in Jameson's summary, the denial that 'a sequence of historical events or texts and artifacts' may be 'rewritten in terms of some deeper, underlying and more "fundamental" narrative'. This is resisted by appeal to the notion of the 'secular scripture':

Romance now again seems to offer the possibility of sensing other historical rhythms, and of demonic or Utopian transformations of a real now unshakably set in place; and Frye is surely not wrong to assimilate the salvational perspective of romance to a reexpression of Utopian longings, a renewed meditation on the Utopian community, a reconquest . . . of some feeling for a salvational future.

The association of Marxism and romance therefore does not discredit the former so much as it explains the persistence and vitality of the latter, which Frye takes to be the ultimate source and paradigm of all storytelling. On this view, the oral tales of tribal society, the fairy tales that are the irrepressible

> voice and expression of the underclasses of the great systems of domination, adventure stories and melodrama, and the popular or mass culture of our own time are all syllables and broken fragments of some single immense story.
>
> (Jameson 1981: 104–5)

The inspiration of Frye pervades the whole of Jameson's lengthy book, and this intuition of a single story recurs frequently. Thus we are told: 'the human adventure is one'. Again: historical events 'recover their original urgency for us only if they are retold within the unity of a single great collective story' and 'only if they are grasped as vital episodes in a single vast unfinished plot' (Jameson 1981: 19–20). We might say that Jameson represents a new breed of critic, the Marxist myth critic, were it not for the fact that he has been anticipated by the Rickword of 'The Cultural Meaning of May Day'; and we might also mention in passing Christopher Caudwell and Jack Lindsay.

The story or 'human adventure' assumed by *The Political Unconscious* is the myth of deliverance. As we know, in its Marxist version it runs from the Eden of primitive communism to the Jerusalem of mature communism, with the 'fall' into class conflict coming between. Unlike Althusser and most other contemporary Marxists, Jameson makes no apology for the mythic structure of this grand narrative. He consistently invokes the collective, class memory of what has been lost (primitive communism) as a prefiguration of the future (mature communism). Memory and desire are indispensable to Marxism.

The argument of *The Political Unconscious* is complex, but makes perfect sense if the above reflections are borne in mind. It may perhaps be summarised, without too much distortion, in five stages. Firstly, Jameson redefines ideology, not as false consciousness but as a 'strategy of containment'. That is, if ideology is illusion, then it is necessary illusion. In order to function within the given social order, we have to 'repress' history. Here Jameson is explicitly politicising Freud, and also adapting Barthes's analysis of 'myth' (actually, ideology) as the presentation of the cultural and historical as natural and eternal. Secondly, Jameson sees history as 'what hurts': that is why we repress it. But to this he adds that it is also a site of contradictions. On the one hand there is the 'hurt' of present class oppression and alienation. On the other hand, there is the 'hope' of a collective, non-oppressive future. The key to both is political revolution, which would remove the oppression and establish the collectivity, but this very need has to be repressed by anyone seeking to survive in her society as it stands. Thirdly, however, Jameson insists that class consciousness itself is by its very nature collective, involving a sense of solidarity. As such, it prefigures, no matter how dimly, the ideal of a communal future. It is, in short, not only ideological but utopian. Fourthly, narrative is a 'socially symbolic act'. That is, like Lévi-Strauss's myth, it resolves the real contradictions of history in imaginative form. In doing so, it allows us to deal provisionally with the 'hurt' and the 'hope', neither of which will go away for long. Fifthly, interpretation is always able to read any given narrative as articulating not only ideology (the repression of the need for revolution) but also utopia (the anticipation of collectivity).

Now let us situate this argument more exactly in terms of influence. We have already mentioned Frye. But it should also be stressed that Jameson is drawing on the ideas of the German philosopher Ernst Bloch (1885–1977), and in particular his apocalyptic version of the Marxist myth of deliverance. The author of the massive work of speculation, *The Principle of Hope* (1959), Bloch argued throughout his career that Marxism is an unapologetically utopian vision of history. Against vulgar interpretations of Marx's work, which reduced it to a mechanical materialism, his Marxism was explicitly a narrative projection of the future. Basing his thinking on not only Marx but also the Bible, and in particular the Book of Revelation, he was fascinated by the tension between the already and the not yet, and he saw Marxism as the secular expression of the latter principle. Hence, no matter how oppressive the given political system might be, and no matter how repressed the vision of an alternative might seem to be, the not yet would somehow find expression in collective fantasy. This could take the form of fairy tale, film or fiction, but the seeds of the future were always implicit in them. In other words, mythic thinking was not to be explained away as reactionary, but was to be celebrated for its utopian potential. Jameson endorses this radical approach to genre:

> Thus, for instance, Bloch's reading of the fairy tale, with its magical wish-fulfilments and its Utopian fantasies of plenty and the *pays de Cocagne*, restores the dialogical and antagonistic content of this 'form' by exhibiting it as a systematic deconstruction and undermining of the hegemonic aristocratic form of the epic, with its somber ideology of heroism and baleful destiny; thus also the work of Eugene Genovese on black religion restores the vitality of these utterances by reading them, not as the replication of imposed beliefs, but rather as a process whereby the hegemonic Christianity of the slave-owners is appropriated, secretly emptied of its content and subverted to the transmission of quite different oppositional and coded messages.
>
> (Jameson 1981: 86)

Nor do we have to confine the utopian dimension of literature to popular narrative. No matter how far a particular literary text might seem to be committed to preserving the status quo, it can always be read with a view to the potential of the not yet. Jameson, fusing the ideas of both *The Principle of Hope* and Frye's *Anatomy*, declares that 'all class consciousness of whatever type is Utopian in so far as it expresses the unity of a collectivity' in an imaginative form:

> The achieved collectivity or organic group of whatever kind –

oppressors fully as much as oppressed – is Utopian not in itself, but only insofar as all such collectivities are themselves *figures* for the ultimate concrete collective life of an achieved Utopia or classless society. Now we are in a better position to understand how even hegemonic or ruling-class culture and ideology are Utopian, not in spite of their instrumental function to secure and perpetuate class privilege and power, but rather precisely because their function is also in and of itself the affirmation of collective solidarity.

(Jameson 1981: 291)

Here we might provide the example of Edmund Spenser's *The Fairie Queene*, Book I, which we have already referred to as a reactionary version of apocalyptic narrative. Jameson would argue that such a text could still be recuperated for revolutionary thought. It celebrates what can be achieved by co-operation: the Red Cross Knight does not work alone, but is aided by Una as much as he aids her, and is also guided throughout his quest by the figure of Prince Arthur. Moreover, any narrative which concerns the victory over the forces of chaos and the reaffirmation of paradisal existence (Eden being saved from the dragon) cannot help but inspire dreams of a better, more equitable world. Again, a modernist work like *The Waste Land*, while it may be seen as the expression of reactionary pessimism, might also persuasively be read, with its evocation of fertility myth and of the quest for the Grail, as a gesture towards a new, non-alienated life.

Thus Jameson affirms 'The Dialectic of Utopia and Ideology', in the words of his conclusion's title. Anticipating the formulations of Paul Ricoeur, he also harks back to those of Kenneth Burke. Indeed, it is to Burke that Jameson owes his concept of narrative as a 'socially symbolic act'. Here is Burke in 1941: 'Critical and imaginative works are answers to questions posed by the situation in which they arose. They are not merely answers, they are *strategic* answers, *stylized* answers.' Thus literature is 'symbolic action'. It is a 'strategy' deployed in a 'situation'. Of course, 'there is a difference, and a radical difference, between building a house and writing a poem about building a house'. One must distinguish between 'practical' and 'symbolic' acts. But the point is that the latter is still an 'act' (Burke 1989: 77–9). Here is Jameson forty years later:

> Kenneth Burke's play of emphases, in which a symbolic act is on the one hand affirmed as a genuine act, albeit on the symbolic level, while on the other it is registered as an act which is 'merely' symbolic, its resolutions imaginary ones that leave the real untouched, suitably demonstrates the ambiguous status of art and culture.
>
> (Jameson 1981: 81)

Jameson is deploying Burke's terminology in order to correct the vulgar or reductive Marxism which views the literary text as a simple reflection of its social and historical 'context'. What he proposes rather is that the literary text is the rewriting of a 'subtext' (Jameson 1981: 81).

We might extrapolate from Jameson's speculations as follows. Frazer explains the periodic sacrifice of a representative of the fertility god as a 'magical' event. The action is meant to ensure the revival of the crops; in an agricultural society, the community relies on the seasonal cycle of vegetation. Frazer points out that the act does not achieve its end, since magic is a false kind of science. Nevertheless, we might say, it is important imaginatively, since it enables the community to affirm itself through ritual and myth. Moreover, both the ritual and the myth offer a means of dealing with intolerable problems such as scarcity and the threat of death, and also of justifying social hierarchy, the god being embodied in the king. They are 'symbolic acts', respectively acting out and narrating a crucial drama, the subtext of which is the 'hurt' of history, whether under the aspect of survival or of social conflict (Dowling 1984: 124–6). A literary example might be

Shelley's poem 'Adonais' (1821), which is a pastoral elegy to his friend, the poet Keats. Based on the myth of Adonis, the dying and reviving god, the poem is merely 'symbolic' in the sense that no matter how much Shelley weeps, his friend will not return from the land of the dead; and that is the burden of the poem itself, to an extent. But 'Adonais' is nonetheless an 'action', which asserts Keats's lasting value as a poet in defiance of those reviewers whose hostility contributed to his early death. History, in the form of philistine bourgeois culture, is both acknowledged and opposed. Another literary example might be Mark Twain's *Huckleberry Finn* (1884), a novel whose very plot concedes that victories over institutional racism are likely to be exceptional, indeed unusual. However, it still acts symbolically upon the problem of oppression by means of the device of the innocent narrator (Huck querying the so-called common sense of his day), the structure of quest romance (Huck and the slave Jim escaping down the Mississippi) and the symbolism of their friendship (Huck preferring damnation with Jim to the salvation favoured by white racists). The 'hope' gets expressed as well as the 'hurt'.

Jameson's 'Dialectic of Utopia and Ideology', then, with its understanding that a challenge to the present and a prefiguration of the future is always implicit, might suggest a position roughly analogous with radical typology. Certainly, in his discussion of traditional interpretations of the Bible, he would seem to reject allegory, in so far as that is perceived as a means of closing off the promise of the scriptures. In Chapter 1 of *The Political Unconscious* Jameson considers 'the medieval system' of interpretation, that method of analysis formulated by St Thomas Aquinas among others, and thoroughly familiar to Dante. It distinguished between the four 'levels' or 'senses' of meaning to be discovered in any Biblical episode: the 'literal' (the historical event narrated); the 'allegorical' (what it tells us about Christ, 'allegory' here being a synonym for 'orthodox typology'); the 'moral' (the relevance for the individual believer); and the 'anagogical' (the spiritual significance). While the notion of 'levels' implies stasis, the four-stage sequence suggests dynamism. Jameson explicitly emphasises the latter. Applying this mode of analysis to the primary myth of deliverance, the story of Moses' leading the exodus of the Hebrews, he shows how each level generates the next, running from the past of the Old Testament to the past of the New, and thence via the present of the reader to the future of humanity. The fourth level is thus the final 'horizon' of interpretation. For him the 'anagogical' does not denote some vague, mystical conjecture, but is the moment 'in which the text undergoes its ultimate rewriting in terms of the destiny of the human race as a whole, Egypt then coming to prefigure that long purgatorial suffering of earthly history from which the second coming of Christ and the Last Judgment come as the final release'. That is, the 'historical or collective dimension' is thus attained once again; only now, 'from the story of a particular people it has been transformed into universal history and the destiny of humankind as a whole' (Jameson 1981: 30–1). Jameson's stress on 'rewriting' is certainly reminiscent of radical typology, but phrases such as 'universal history' may give us occasion for doubts. These doubts may be confirmed when the medieval system is translated explicitly into Marxist terms, and the senses or levels are made to conform to the theory of the mode of production:

What our preceding discussion of the medieval levels suggests . . . is that this is by no means the whole story, and that to grasp the full degree to which this schema projects an essentially alle-gorical operation, we must enlarge its master code or allegorical key to the point at which the latter becomes a master narrative in its own right; and this point is reached when we become aware that any individual mode of production projects and implies a whole sequence of such modes of production – from primitive communism to capitalism and communism proper

– which constitute the narrative of some properly Marxian 'philosophy of history'.

(Jameson 1981: 33)

Though the motto of *The Political Unconscious*, announced on its first page, is 'Always historicize!', it needs to be read in tension with the above quotation, where temporal sequence is immediately translated into a 'philosophy of history'. Again, consider another statement which is made barely a page into the book, concerning 'metacommentary': 'Interpretation is here construed as an essentially allegorical act, which consists in rewriting a given text in terms of a particular interpretive master-code.' Specifically, 'Marxism is here conceived as that "untranscendable horizon" that subsumes such apparently antagonistic or incommensurable critical operations' as psychoanalysis, myth criticism and structuralism, 'at once cancelling them and preserving them' (Jameson 1981: 10). That is, however Bloch may rewrite Marxism as a myth of the not yet, of permanent possibility, Jameson ultimately insists on closure and finality. There may be many fascinating ways of imagining the future within history, but only Marxism can comprehend history. As Robert Young explains:

Even though Marxist criticism must now enter the marketplace as interpretation rather than, as in the old days, through an invocation of its higher knowledge in the form of History and Truth, it is still a superior form of interpretation. For unlike all the others it does not actually have to compete with its rivals because, according to its dialectical logic, it can both incorporate them and transcend them. What at first, then, looked like an abandonment of traditional Marxist notions of History and Truth was in fact only a first move in bringing them back via the meta-claim of interpretive absolutism and history as transcendence.

(Young 1990: 103)

In short, just as with orthodox Christianity, 'the meaning precedes the interpretation', and all interpretation is 'simply a matter of translation into a master code' (Young 1990: 107). Jameson's choice of the paradigm of the myth of deliverance has resulted in a mythic reading that insists on closure and finality.

In this light Jameson may be seen to differ not only from Bloch but also from Burke and Frye. Burke argues that 'hierarchy' is always open to the 'comic corrective', and that there is no system which is not susceptible to 'perspective by incongruity'. He further argues that such a corrective or perspective must always be immanent, since there is no transcendent position from which to look down on the whole of history. Perfection is always a projection. There being no absolute truth, we are each of us only able to view the world through a particular 'terministic screen', which sets limits to what can be seen: 'Even if any given terminology is a *reflection* of reality, by its very nature as a terminology it must be a *selection* of reality; and to this extent it must function also as a *deflection* of reality' (Burke 1966: 45). So much is suggested by Jameson's 'strategy of containment', except that Jameson believes that his own 'strategy', namely Marxism, is exempt from the historical limits it depicts and diagnoses. Similarly, where Frye gives priority to 'the order of words', so that cosmos and history alike become cultural constructions, Jameson insists that history at least exists in its own right before it becomes mythologized. Deferring to Althusser on this point, he accepts that history might best be conceived as 'an absent cause' which, like Freud's unconscious, cannot be known directly but only through its effects:

> We would therefore propose the following revised formulation: that history is *not* a text, not a narrative, master or otherwise, but that, as an absent cause, it is inaccessible to us except in textual form, and that our approach to it and to the Real

itself necessarily passes through its prior textualization, its narrativization in the political unconscious.

(Jameson 1981: 35)

Reading this quotation in isolation, we might hesitate to label Jameson's position as either realism or non-realism, but the above insistence on Marxism as 'allegory' and on the need for a 'master-code' must surely rule out non-realism. What we have here, then, is a variant on realism which avoids literalism but which will concede the minimum to pragmatism and perspectivism. It is akin to the position advocated by Stephen Ross White in his own reaction against Don Cupitt's theology: that is, 'critical realism' (White 1994: 207). Though this usage should not be confused with that of Georg Lukács in his discussion of fiction, where 'critical' refers to the judgement made on capitalist society by certain novels approved by him, we may validly infer a connection. For Lukács, realism is the form which allows author and reader to discover and interrogate the essence of an historical era, dominated by one main mode of production, and so to infer the movement of history itself, conceived as a sequence of modes of production. Similarly, the idea for White is that one may continue to invoke the real, even while one admits that it is only articulated and known indirectly. Because one's own mode of interpretation is transcendent, one can continue to act as if one were in possession of the absolute truth rather than a provisional meaning. Jameson is in accord with Lukács and White.

But it would be unfair to dismiss Jameson's Marxist myth-criticism on the grounds that its assumption of totality is in itself totalitarian. Jameson's skill as an interpreter of narrative is such that we take away from *The Political Unconscious* and his other works the sense, not of remorseless reduction, but of continuing surprise. His understanding of myth is profound, and his ability to read literary texts mythically is agile and endlessly suggestive. We have already referred in Part I to his reading of *Ulysses. The*

Political Unconscious itself contains long and intriguing inter-pretations, too long and intriguing to be summarised neatly here, of classic texts such as Conrad's *Lord Jim* (Jameson 1981: 206 ff.). It is as if, despite his adherence to the closure and finality of the Marxist grand narrative, with its attendant allegorical master-code, the spirit of his criticism is permanent possibility – that of radical typology.

Thus in his response to the phenomenon of postmodernity, given initially only three years after the publication of *The Political Unconscious*, he does not simply reassert the validity of Marxism in the face of what he calls 'the cultural logic of late capitalism'. He diagnoses the condition with the same enthusiasm as he might want to reserve only for the utopian aspect of traditional and modern narratives. Richard Kearney suggests that the postmodern condition brings with it a shift to the metaphor of culture as 'a labyrinth of mirrors', in which nothing is stable or certain: a con-tinuing intertextual play of images (Kearney 1988: 253). Jameson knows and understands this, and he acknowledges the radical difference between Van Gogh's painting of peasant shoes, redolent of authenticity and depth, and Warhol's 'Diamond Dust Shoes', self-referential and wilfully superficial (Jameson 1984: 58–60). His answer is not to invoke the 'reality' of class struggle and the 'truth' of Marxism, but to risk a wager, to propose a tentative clue to the labyrinth, potentially no less effective than Ariadne's thread. He calls this clue an 'aesthetic of cognitive mapping': that would be a 'new political art' which would have to begin to negotiate 'the world space of international capital' at the same time as it attempts 'a breakthrough to some as yet unimaginable new mode of representing this last' (Jameson 1984: 92). It is as if we were being reminded that the Marxist myth of deliverance, that 'vast unfinished plot', is nothing without the permanent potential of creative rewriting and radical improvisation.

IN THE LABYRINTH

It is in the midst of the postmodern 'labyrinth of mirrors' that Marina Warner begins the second of her 1994 Reith Lectures, *Managing Monsters*. She recalls her recent experience at the 'Future Entertainment Show', where she found herself to be one of the few female visitors. The place was packed with teenage boys and young men playing video games: games like 'Streets of Rage', 'Mortal Kombat', 'Street Fighter', 'Zombie Apocalypse' and 'Splatterhouse'. In each of these 'the hero slays monsters': 'Just as Jason and his Argonauts did or Hercules and his Twelve Labours – indeed some of the games quote classical adventures and their pantheons.' What more is involved is hard to discern: the narrative richness of the ancient paradigm of hero myth has been forgotten, and all we have is the moment when 'the hero busts his way through' (Warner 1994: 17–18). Sophisticated techno-logically, we seem to have become naive mythologically. In the face of this chaos of perfunctory narratives, Warner thus has to attempt her own kind of 'cognitive mapping'.

From the Babylonian creation myth, featuring Marduk's battle with Tiamat, through Greek hero myths such as Theseus and the minotaur, to the romance of St George and the dragon, myth and monstrosity have always been linked. Warner traces the word 'monster' back to two Latin words, one of which means 'show' and the other of which means 'warn':

> a myth shows something, it's a story spoken to a purpose, it issues a warning, it gives an account which advises and tells often by bringing into play showings of fantastical shape and invention – monsters. Myths define enemies and aliens and in conjuring them up they say who we are and what we want, they tell stories to impose structure and order.
>
> (Warner 1994: 19)

That being so, what do contemporary monsters tell us about ourselves, particularly the role of men? Warner's lecture is called 'Boys Will Be Boys: The Making of the Male', and it explores a disturbing shift in attitudes. If the key narrative is that of hero myth, then we have witnessed a change in our conception of heroism. Moving back from the contemporary model of the hero as unthinking aggressor, she demonstrates the relevance of other models, one modern and one ancient. Her texts are *Frankenstein* and the *Odyssey*.

Though Warner's focus is on hero myth, she is also interested in variations on paradigms: thus her choice of *Frankenstein* (1818) is interesting because it is itself a radical exploration of two inherited models. It is both a modern hero myth, with its protagonist as scientific experimenter, and a modern creation myth, with its story of the construction of a new creature by human agency. Thus it rewrites two stories: that of Prometheus, maker of humanity, as told in ancient Greece (in the eighth century BC) by Hesiod and that of the Book of Genesis, as mediated by Milton's *Paradise Lost*. Warner, acknowledging this dual legacy, explores the central shift of emphasis from antiquity to modernity, whereby the human being arrogantly takes all the initiative. But she demonstrates that Mary Shelley's achievement is not only to rewrite ancient myths, but to challenge modern thinking. In particular the novel queries the supremacy of male rationality: 'Mary Shelley grasped the likelihood that a man might make a monster in his own image and then prove incapable of taking responsibility for it.' Thus a crucial episode is that in which the 'creature' demands its independent rights, above all that to a mate, and his appalled creator refuses, declaring that he and the monster are 'enemies'. Shelley exposes this modern double-bind: the monster is an emanation of the male mind, but the male mind can only cope with it by hostility. And it is this hostility, Warner reminds us, which alone gets expressed in contemporary video narratives; whereas the novel presents us with the monster's own poignant case. 'Current tales of conflict and extermination never hear the monster say: "I am malicious, because I am miserable." Or, "Make me happy, and I shall again be virtuous." The phrases sound absurd, because we're so accustomed to expect the hero to have no other way of managing monsters than slaying them' (Warner 1994: 21–2). We are thus invited to read Mary Shelley's modern, exploratory myth not only as a rewriting of ancient paradigms but as a challenge to our own complacency and aggression.

Similarly, Warner reminds us that what has been taken over from Greek hero myth and epic has been the model of the brutal combatant. We have to reread the ancient paradigm in order to see how far we have simplified the notion of heroism:

> In Homer, Odysseus tells the Cyclops that his name is Nobody. So, when Odysseus blinds the Cyclops in his one eye, the giant howls for help to his father the god of the sea and the other Olympians. But all the gods hear is his cry, 'Nobody has blinded me.' And so they do nothing.
>
> This trick from the *Odyssey* is literally one of the oldest in the book. The hero who lives by his wits survives in countless hard luck, Puss in Boots-style stories . . . .
>
> Charlie Chaplin, and even Woody Allen have worked this groove, the heroic pathetic. But a gleeful use of cunning and high spirits against brute force, a reliance on subterfuge have almost faded from heroic myth today. In the prevailing popular concept of masculinity, as reflected in comics, rock bands, street fashion, Clint Eastwood or Arnold Schwarzenegger movies, the little man, the riddler or trickster has yielded before the type of warrior hero, the paradigm of the fittest survivor.
>
> (Warner 1994: 25)

Moreover, where Greek heroes did slavishly follow the logic of violence, they were not presented as ideal figures but as 'tragic warnings'. They were 'objects of debate, not models' (Warner

1994: 27). This possibility is not allowed for in the scope of 'Splatterhouse' and 'Cannon Fodder'.

However, Warner is not pessimistic. The title of her lecture series suggests that we need not think of monsters as things to 'manage' simply by slaying. Her point is that we have the choice, indeed the obligation, to 'manage' them in another sense: that is, acknowledge them, negotiate with them, interpret them, query them. Here we may think of Jung's process of individuation, which involves facing and incorporating the power of the shadow, our own repressed psyche. Or we may think of Lévi-Strauss's analysis of the resolution of contradictions in the Oedipus story, with the monstrous signifying the earthly origins with which humanity has to come to terms. But Warner differs from them in her insistence that monsters, like myths, are primarily historical. That is to say, the most important thing to do is to interrogate the form which monstrosity is taking in our time. In so far as it becomes merely the alien enemy, the object of mindless terror and violence, we need to remember that 'if monsters are made, not given, they can be unmade, too' (Warner 1994: 31). Here we get some sense of Warner's overall purpose, not only in the Reith Lectures but throughout her career. In *Alone of All Her Sex* she considers 'The Myth and Cult of the Virgin Mary' in relation to early goddess-worship as well as the courtly myth-making of the twelfth-century Troubadour poets. *Monuments and Maidens* includes a reading of Margaret Thatcher, the 'iron lady' of British politics, as Boadicea. In *From the Beast to the Blonde* she encompasses Rapunzel, Marilyn Monroe and (the singer) Madonna in the space of a few paragraphs. That is, she offers a history of myth in terms of its rereading, its rewriting, its re-creating. She is deeply conscious of the ambiguous power of stories: their capacity to enchant can be both life-affirming and destructive. Our obligation is to be both receptive and vigilant. Realising that myth is always going to be open to change, we must participate in the operation: 'I believe the process of understanding and clarification ...

can give rise to newly told stories, can sew and weave and knit different patterns into the social fabric and that this is a continuous enterprise for everyone to take part in' (Warner 1994: xiv). What for Jameson is a source of regret, namely the loss of a sense of originality and authenticity, is for her a sign of constant renewal, of cultural life. She states this clearly as follows: 'Every telling of a myth is a part of that myth; there is no Ur-version, no authentic prototype, no true account' (Warner 1994: 8). Again:

> Myths offer a lens which can be used to see human identity in its social and cultural context – they can lock us up in stock reactions, bigotry and fear, but they're not immutable, and by unpicking them, the stories can lead to others. Myths convey values and expectations which are always evolving, in the process of being formed, but – and this is fortunate – never set so hard they cannot be changed again.
>
> (Warner 1994: 14)

That is a fair summary of the principle we have been calling radical typology. We must trust, we are told, in the very power of myth to change and, in the process, to change us. 'Intertextuality' is not the problem but the solution, if positively understood. For, unlike Lévi-Strauss and Barthes, she does not believe that myth is something that happens behind our backs, as it were: she insists that we have the capacity, as tellers and retellers, interpreters and reinterpreters, to maintain the interaction of myth and history.

Myths will always need retelling and reinterpreting, and the women's movement, feminist and postfeminist, has made striking contributions to this process. Thus Elinor W. Gadon views the myth of Theseus and the minotaur as a story justifying the destruction of Minoan matriarchy and goddess-worship. When the patriarchal Mycenaeans invaded Crete, bringing their sky father Zeus with them, they sought to discredit, but also incorporate, such rituals as 'bull leaping' which the Cretans had conducted in a 'labyrinth' sacred to the goddess. In telling the tale of the killing of the minotaur (half-bull, dwelling in the womb of the earth) they celebrated the suppression of Minoan female-centred religion (Gadon 1989: 97–107). Again, Hélène Cixous takes the figure of monstrosity in the undoubtedly male-oriented Perseus myth, and celebrates the female monster whom the hero has to behead. For her 'The Laugh of the Medusa' is an emblem of a bisexuality which evades sexual distinction and domination, and she proposes a new kind of writing which subverts essentialism and expresses the multiplicity of desire (Cixous 1980: 253–4).

Similarly, interpretation must be reinterpreted. On the whole, Freud's influence has been an anxious one. Kate Millett set the agenda when she declared him to be 'beyond question the strongest individual counterrevolutionary force in the ideology of sexual politics' (Millett 1969: 178); but Juliet Mitchell, Jacqueline Rose and others have argued in favour of the theory of the Oedipus complex in so far as it implies that sexual identity is a cultural construct rather than a stable, biological essence (Moi 1985: 28). Jung has had an easier passage, given his more positive view of the female. But 'feminist archetypal theory' has had to acknowledge such regrettable tendencies as that of associating the male with 'thought' and the female with 'feeling'. Again, the term 'archetype' has had to be redefined as the 'tendency to form and reform images in relation to certain kinds of repeated experience', and so as varying from culture to culture and from individual to individual, rather than as an eternal and universal form (Lauter and Rupprecht 1985: 13–14).

Some of the most important acts of mythic reading inspired by the women's movement have been works of fiction. In the novels of Margaret Atwood, for instance, mythopoeia (forging new possibilities of narrative for women) and mythography (interrogating the dominant male narrative) are brilliantly achieved at the same time. Particularly impressive is *The Handmaid's Tale* (1985). This is presented as the memoir of 'Offred', or 'Of-Fred', the eponymous female hero, who lives in the near-future fundamentalist republic of Gilead, in what was New England, where her job is to bear children for state officials whose marriages are barren. There the Bible, particularly the Old Testament, is taken literally, and used to justify the oppression of women. Offred tell us about her 'placement' at the home of 'the Commander', a high-ranking government official, where she has to take the place of Serena, the commander's wife, during the act of sexual intercourse. While recounting this part of her life, she also wonders what has become of her own husband Luke and their child. We also hear about her friend Moira, who rebels against the system, only to end up working in the state-run brothel, 'Jezebel's'. Offred herself dreams of getting away from Gilead, and at the end of the memoir we are not sure whether the commander's chauffeur Nick has effected her flight over the Canadian border. For, entering the van which he has brought for her, she herself does not know whether she is escaping or going to prison: 'And so I step up, into the darkness within; or else the light' (Atwood 1996: 307). The novel concludes with some 'Historical Notes', a partial transcript from an academic conference on Offred's narrative, held in 2195, when her world is already past. The keynote address by 'Professor Pieixoto' consists of a brusque and insensitive commentary on the text we have just read, which shows he scarcely understands it. But his last sentence, which for the participants in the conference is simply a conventional token, also significantly forms the last sentence of Atwood's novel: 'Are there any questions?' (Atwood 1996: 324). This open-ended novel invites us to query the way in which narratives are constructed and interpreted, and above all how one narrative gains precedence over others.

Thus, though we can easily categorise *The Handmaid's Tale* in literary-critical terms, what merits attention is the way it deconstructs and reconstructs myth. Strictly speaking, Atwood's novel belongs to the category of 'dystopia' or 'anti-utopia'. But as Northrop Frye observes, this phase of satire carries its own mythic directive: it 'presents human life in terms of largely unrelieved bondage. Its settings feature prisons, madhouses, lynching mobs, and places of execution.' That is, with this form of narrative, which Frye takes to be an extreme form of the ironic mode, we are granted a full-scale 'demonic' vision, the complement of the 'apocalyptic'. This ironic myth, of which Orwell's *Nineteen Eighty-Four* is representative, depicts 'the nightmare of social tyranny', often featuring 'the use of parody-religious symbols suggesting some form of Satan or Antichrist worship' (Frye 1971: 238). Atwood, who studied under Frye at the University of Toronto, would seem to have taken the full measure of this insight, and her novel may be seen as a conscious exercise in ironic mythopoeia. For 'Gilead', named after the place where the patriarch Jacob set up his 'heap of stones' and established his household, is dedicated to the worship of God the Father, the deity of law and male authority – Blake's Urizen. In the name of this patriarchal God, Offred and her fellow Handmaids are held, pending 'placements', in a prison camp which was once part of Harvard University: they are denied knowledge and given dogma. The Bible is reduced to arid formulae, mainly concerning the necessity for women to obey men and the obligation to breed. The soldiers of Gilead's army are called 'Angels', and the policemen are called 'Guardians of the Faith'. Apart from mass-religious ceremonies known as 'Prayvaganzas', Handmaids are expected to participate in the violence of public, mob executions, euphemistically known as 'Salvagings'. And all the while, for every 'Offred' there is an 'Ofglen' who has instructions to spy on her counterpart for signs of deviance from, or doubt about, the state.

But parodying religion is not the only point of *The Handmaid's Tale*. What is being interrogated is the imposition of the Word upon words, of the illusion of truth on the power of fantasy. The enemy is totalitarianism, the attempt to subject people to one conception of totality. What Atwood shows us in Offred is someone struggling to maintain the profane imagination against the dead weight of doctrine, sacred or otherwise. Significantly, the Handmaids are told that the slogan 'From each according to her ability; to each according to his needs' comes from St Paul, when it actually comes from Marx (Atwood 1996: 127). The two grand narratives, the Marxist and the Biblical, are equally false when turned into absolute truth. So Offred, in resisting the deadly totality of Gilead – deadly because believed in – has to reaffirm the permanent possibility of myth. In resisting the false and oppressive perfection of dogma, she needs to build up a universe through art, and specifically through narrative. The 'demonic' world she knows all too well. The 'apocalyptic' world (in Frye's positive sense) is symbolised by Serena's garden. It gives Offred 'a sense of buried things bursting upwards, wordlessly, into the light, as if to point, to say: Whatever is silenced will clamour to be heard, though silently.' Indeed: 'Goddesses are possible now and the air suffuses with desire' (Atwood 1996: 161–2). Her whole narrative is, in the strict sense, a romance: she is on a quest. This being an ironic narrative, the quest is incomplete, and what we are left with at the end is the vivid memory of conflict and struggle. But in tension with that is the possibility, symbolised by the garden, that a life beyond this nightmare death-in-life may be found. Thus, when we call this novel a dystopia we mean two things. On the one hand it satirises a regime which functions according to an ideology which is already present (the New Right, with its fundamentalist Christianity), taken to its logical conclusions. On the other hand, it offers hope for the future, since such an indictment would have little force without some counter-sense of possibility, and so a tacit dialectic of ideology and utopia. Thus *The Handmaid's Tale*, as a mythopoeic novel, is a work which implies both the 'demonic' and the 'apocalyptic' dimensions. It is about the potential, the power of resistance and affirmation, implicit in imagination itself.

Atwood cannot be accused of treating this potential in a facile manner, as the whole novel engages with the most important conflict and struggle of all, that over language. To quote one of her own poems: 'A word after a word/after a word is power' (Atwood 1981: 64). The task, then, is to keep word following word. Hence the importance of the closing sentence of the novel. It is important that an implicit rejoinder to Professor Pieixeto be thought possible. For he represents the aridity of *logos*, un-comprehending in the face of *mythos*. Indicatively, he finds the document to be 'in its way eloquent', but 'mute' on important factual matters (Atwood 1996: 323–4).

Just as Gilead does not know how to read the grand narrative of the Bible without turning it into a a handbook of dogma, so the professor does not know how to read the vulnerable and tentative narration before him, this 'Handmaid's tale', without turning it into an object to be explained away. In challenging this systematic ignorance Atwood's novel may be said to exemplify the paradoxical power of Gianni Vattimo's 'fragile' imagination:

> Numerous peoples and cultures have taken to the world stage, and it has become impossible to believe that history is a unilinear process directed towards a *telos*. The realization of the universality of history has made universal history impossible. Consequently, the idea that the course of history could be thought of as enlightenment, as the liberation of reason from the shadows of mythical knowledge, has lost its legitimacy . . . . When demythologization itself is revealed as myth, myth regains legitimacy, but only within the frame of a generally 'weakened' experience of truth. The presence of myth in our culture does not represent an alternative or opposing movement to modernization, but is rather its natural outcome, its destination, at least thus far. The demythologization of demythologization, moreover, may be taken as the true moment of transition from the modern to the postmodern.
>
> (Vattimo 1992: 39, 42)

The way forward is that commended by Nietzsche in *The Gay Science*: 'to know one is dreaming and to go on dreaming'. These words are 'an expression of a destiny that belongs to our culture, a destiny that can also be denoted by another term, namely *secularization*':

> The secularization of the European spirit of the modern age does not consist solely in the exposure and demystification of the errors of religion, but also in the survival of these 'errors' in different, and in some sense degraded, forms. A secularized culture is not one that has simply left the religious elements of its tradition behind, but one that continues to live them as traces, as hidden and distorted models that are nonetheless profoundly present.
>
> (Vattimo 1992: 40)

What is being commended here is not the abandonment of the idea of the sacred, but its absorption into the profane or 'secularized' imagination. The ambition of antiquity, to legitimate myth by reference to metaphysical foundations, must go. But so must the ambition of modernity, to discredit myth by reference to scientific foundations. Richard Kearney has summarised Vattimo's alternative, his postmodernist mythopoeia. It involves:

> retaining myth as a secular interplay of multifaceted meanings; an interplay which dramatizes our cultural memories and traditions as historical interpretations rather than idolizing them as timeless dogmas. The post-modern 'overcoming' of myth which Vattimo counsels . . . proposes to salvage myth in the transposed form of an ironically distanced or diluted reinterpretation. By not taking itself too seriously (that is, literally), myth can be taken seriously once again. Whence the curious paradox: it is precisely when the modern cult of 'demythization' is itself unmasked as a myth (an Enlightenment myth of

absolute Reason) that the mythic imaginary can recover its legitimacy. But this legitimacy resides in the very acknowledgement of the *limits* of myth – its inherent modesty and *faiblesse* as an experience of truth. The weakness of myth is its strength. Its disclaimer to absolute truth is its claim to partial truth – the only kind we, as finite historical interpreters, can ever presume to possess.

(Kearney 1991: 183–4)

Modest as the scope of myth now is, it may yet overcome the modern 'opposition between rationalism and irrationalism' and so open the way to a new kind of thought (Vattimo 1992: 43). Kearney relates this suggestion to Ricoeur's 'poetics of the possible', and regards both as opening up an 'ethics of the possible':

Post-modernism, understood in Vattimo's sense of a non-foundational and non-functionalist theory of interpretation, solicits an ethical task of remembering that is not a simple repetition of tradition but its joyous re-creation. Such remembering emancipates tradition from servile conformism, transposing it into a historical transmission of overtures to possible modes of being-in-the-world.

(Kearney 1991: 185–6)

That is, the very act of remembering and re-creating the sacred narratives of the past in secular, aesthetic terms would be an act of emancipation: not in the Enlightenment sense of rational progress, but in a new spirit of 'ludic imagining'. While Kearney does not spell out this ethics here, we can infer from the rest of his argument that it is an ethics of 'otherness'. This would be meant in a triple sense. Firstly, the myth recalls and projects an 'other' world. Secondly, the myth reminds us that there is always something else, something 'other', to be said or imagined. Thirdly, the myth, as a play of past paradigm and future possibility, gives expression to the 'other', to those persons and causes excluded from the present hierarchy. Thus we might come to understand myth, 'fragile' as it is, as a disclosure rather than as a dogma: as a narrative whose potential always evades the given order, with its illusion of truth. Though we will continue to be 'rotten with perfection', in Burke's phrase, we may come to see that it is the task of myth constantly to imply, but always to resist, completion. Myth might then be appreciated as that narrative mode of understanding which involves a continuing dialectic of same and other, of memory and desire, of ideology and utopia, of hierarchy and horizon, and of sacred and profane.

BIBLIOGRAPHY

Abrams, M.H. (1971) *Natural Supernaturalism: Tradition and Revolution in Romantic Literature*, New York: Norton.

Ackerman, Robert (1990) *J.G. Frazer: His Life and Work*, Cambridge: Cambridge University Press.

Allen, Don Cameron (1970) *Mysteriously Meant: The Rediscovery of Pagan Symbolism and Allegorical Interpretation in the Renaissance*, Baltimore: Johns Hopkins University Press.

Altizer, Thomas J.J. (1963) *Mircea Eliade and the Dialectic of the Sacred*, Westport, Connecticut: Greenwood Press.

—— (1967) *The New Apocalypse: The Radical Christian Vision of William Blake*, Ann Arbor: Michigan State University Press.

—— (1985) *History as Apocalypse*, New York: Albany.

—— (1990) *Genesis and Apocalypse: A Theological Voyage toward Authentic Christianity*, Louisville, Kentucky: John Knox Press.

——, Beardslee, William, A. and Young, J. Harvey (eds) (1962) *Truth, Myth and Symbol*, New York: Prentice-Hall.

Atwood, Margaret (1981) *True Stories*, New York: Simon & Schuster.

—— (1996) *The Handmaid's Tale*, London: Virago.

Auerbach, Erich (1968) *Mimesis: The Representation of Reality in Western Literature*, Princeton: Princeton University Press.

—— (1984) *Scenes from the Drama of European Literature*, Manchester: Manchester University Press.

Barnaby, Karin and D'Acierno, Pellegrino (eds) (1990) *C.G. Jung and the Humanities*, London: Routledge.

Barthes, Roland (1973) *Mythologies*, London: Paladin.

—— (1981) *Image–Music–Text*, ed. S. Heath, New York: Hill & Wang.

Barton, John (1984) *Reading the Old Testament: Method in Biblical Study*, London: Darton, Longman & Todd.

Bell, Michael (1972) *Primitivism*, London: Methuen.

Beltz, Walter (1983) *God and the Gods: Myths of the Bible*, Harmondsworth: Penguin.

Bertens, Hans (1995) *The Idea of the Postmodern: A History*, London: Routledge.

Blackwell, Trevor and Seabrook, Jeremy (1988) *The Politics of Hope*, London: Faber & Faber.

Blake, William (1971) *Complete Writings*, ed. Geoffrey Keynes, London: Oxford University Press.

Brown, Norman O. (1973) *Closing Time*, New York: Random House.

Brunel, Pierre (ed.) *Companion to Literary Myths, Heroes and Archetypes*, London & New York: Routledge.

Bull, Malcolm (ed.) (1995) *Apocalypse Theory and the Ends of the World*, Oxford: Blackwell.

Bultmann, Rudolf (1953) 'The New Testament and Mythology', in H.W. Bartsch (ed.), *Kerygma and Myth: A Theological Debate*, London: SPCK.

Burke, Kenneth (1966) *Language as Symbolic Action: Essays on Life, Literature and Method*, Berkeley: University of California Press.

—— (1970) *The Rhetoric of Religion: Studies in Logology*, Berkeley: University of California Press.

—— (1971) 'Doing and Saying: Thoughts on Myth, Cult and Archetype', *Salmagundi* 7: 100–19.

—— (1989) *On Symbols and Society*, ed. J.R. Gusfield, Chicago: University of Chicago Press.

Campbell, Joseph (1988) *The Hero with a Thousand Faces*, London: Paladin.

Cantor, Paul A. (1984) *Creature and Creator: Myth-making and English Romanticism*, Cambridge: Cambridge University Press.

Cixous, Hélène (1980) 'The Laugh of the Medusa', in E. Marks and I. de Courtivron (eds) *New French Feminism*, Brighton: Harvester.

Clifford, James (1986) (ed.) *Writing Culture: The Poetics and Politics of Ethnography*, Berkeley: University of California Press.

Cohn, Norman (1970) *The Pursuit of the Millennium*, London: Paladin.

—— (1993) *Cosmos, Chaos and the World to Come*, New York: Yale University Press.

Coleridge, S.T. (1971) *Select Poetry and Prose*, ed. Stephen Potter, London: Nonesuch Press.

Conrad, Joseph (1973) *Heart of Darkness*, Harmondsworth: Penguin.

Coppola, Francis Ford (1979) *Apocalypse Now*, USA: Zoetrope.

Coupe, Laurence (1989) 'Freud's *Interpretation of Dreams* and Modern Hermeneutics', in Laurence Spurling (ed) *Sigmund Freud: Critical Approaches*, Routledge, 1989, Vol III, 340–53.

—— (1994) 'Reading for the Myth', *English Review* 4, 4: 6–9.

—— (1995) 'Violence and the Sacred: *Murder in the Cathedral*', *English Review* 6, 2: 28–31.

—— (1997) 'Rewriting the Cosmos: The Radical Vision of William Blake', *English Review* 7, 3: 38–41.

Cowie, Peter (1990) *Coppola*, London: Faber & Faber.

Cupitt, Don (1982) *The World to Come*, London: SCM Press.

—— (1986) *Life Lines*, London: SCM Press.

—— (1990) *Creation out of Nothing*, London: SCM Press.

—— (1991) *What is a Story?*, London: SCM Press.

—— (1992) *The Time Being*, London: SCM Press.

—— (1995) *The Last Philosophy*, London: SCM Press.

Dante Alighieri (1995) *The Portable Dante*, ed. M. Musa, London and New York: Penguin/Viking.

Derrida, Jacques (1982) 'Of an Apocalyptic Tone Recently Adopted in Philosophy', *Semeia* 23: 63–97.

—— (1994) 'Spectres of Marx', *New Left Review* 205: 31–58.

Dickens, Charles (1971) *Bleak House*, Harmondsworth: Penguin.

Docherty, Thomas (ed.) (1993) *Postmodernism: A Reader*, New York and London: Harvester.

The Doors (1992) *The Doors: Lyrics 1965–1971*, London: Omnibus.

Doty, William G. (1986) *Mythography: The Study of Myths and Rituals*, Tuscaloosa: University of Alabama Press.

Dowling, William C. (1984) *Jameson, Althusser, Marx: An Introduction to 'The Political Unconscious'*, London: Methuen.

Eco, Umberto (1989) *The Middle Ages of James Joyce*, London: Hutchinson Radius.

Eliade, Mircea (1958) *Patterns in Comparative Religion*, London: Sheed and Ward.

—— (1968) *Myths, Dreams and Mysteries*, London: Fontana.

—— (1971) *The Myth of the Eternal Return: Or, Cosmos and History*, Princeton: Princeton University Press.

Eliot, T.S. (1934) *After Strange Gods: A Primer of Modern Heresy*, London: Faber & Faber.

—— (1961) *Murder in the Cathedral*, London: Faber & Faber.

—— (1963) *Collected Poems 1909–1962*, London: Faber & Faber.

—— (1964) *The Use of Poetry and the Use of Criticism*, London: Faber & Faber.

—— (1970) *For Lancelot Andrewes: Essays on Style and Order*, London: Faber & Faber.

—— (1975) *Selected Prose*, ed. F. Kermode, London: Faber & Faber.

Feldman, Burton and Richardson, Robert D. (1972) *The Rise of Modern Mythology*, Bloomington: Indiana University Press.

Ferguson, John (1980) *Jesus in the Tide of Time: An Historical Study*, London: Routledge & Kegan Paul.

Fiedler, Leslie (1963) *No! in Thunder: Essays on Myth and Literature*, London: Eyre & Spottiswoode.

Fiorenza, Elisabeth (1985) *The Book of Revelation: Justice and Judgement*, Philadelphia: Fortress Press.

Fowlie, Wallace (1994) *Rimbaud and Jim Morrison: The Rebel as Poet*, London: Souvenir Press.

Frazer, Sir James (1978) *The Illustrated Golden Bough*, ed. Sabine McCormack, London: Macmillan.

Freud, Sigmund (1950) *Collected Papers*, Vol. V, London: Hogarth Press.

—— (1974) *The Interpretation of Dreams*, in *Complete Works*, Vols IV–V, London: Hogarth Press.

—— (1985) *The Origins of Religion*, ed. A. Dickson, Harmondsworth: Penguin.

Frye, Northrop (1965) *A Natural Perspective: The Development of Shakespearean Comedy and Romance*, New York: Harcourt Brace.

—— (1971) *Anatomy of Criticism: Four Essays*, Princeton: Princeton University Press.

—— (1976) *The Secular Scripture: A Study of the Structure of Romance*, Cambridge, Mass.: Harvard University Press.

—— (1978) *Northrop Frye on Culture and Literature*, ed. R. Denham, Chicago: University of Chicago Press.

—— (1981) *T.S. Eliot: An Introduction*, Chicago: University of Chicago Press.

—— (1982) *The Great Code: The Bible and Literature*, London: Routledge & Kegan Paul.

Gadon, Elinor W. (1989) *The Once and Future Goddess: A Symbol for our Time*, New York: Harper Collins.

Geertz, Clifford (1993) *The Interpretation of Cultures: Selected Essays*, London: Fontana.

Girard, René (1977) *Violence and the Sacred*, Baltimore: Johns Hopkins University Press.

Gould, Eric (1981) *Mythical Intentions in Modern Literature*, Princeton: Princeton University Press.

Graf, Fritz (1993) *Greek Myth: An Introduction*, Baltimore: Johns Hopkins University Press.

Grant, Michael (1962) *Myths of the Greeks and Romans*, London: Weidenfeld & Nicolson.

Hellmann, John (1986) *American Myth and the Legacy of Vietnam*, New York: Columbia University Press.

Herr, Michael (1978) *Dispatches*, London: Pan.

Hill, Geoffrey (1985) *Collected Poems*, Harmondsworth: Penguin.

Holm, Jean and Howker, John (eds) (1994) *Myth and History*, London & New York: Pinter.

Hooke, S.H. (1978) *Middle Eastern Mythology*, Harmondsworth: Penguin.

Hopkins, Jerry and Sugerman, Danny (1980) *No One Here Gets Out Alive*, London: Plexus.

Jameson, Fredric (1981) *The Political Unconscious: Narrative as a Socially Symbolic Act*, London: Methuen.

—— (1982) '*Ulysses* in History', in W.J. McCormack and A. Stead (eds), *James Joyce and Modern Literature*, London: Routledge & Kegan Paul.

—— (1984) 'Postmodernism: Or, the Cultural Logic of Late Capitalism', *New Left Review* 146: 53–92.

Jenkyns, Richard (1992) *Classical Epic: Homer and Virgil*, London: Duckworth.

Jewett, Robert and Lawrence, John Shelton (1977) *The American Monomyth*, New York: Doubleday.

Jones, Derek and Handley, Graham (1988) *The Modern World: Ten Great Writers*, London: Channel Four Publications.

Joyce, James (1960) *Ulysses*, London: Bodley Head.

—— (1966) *Finnegans Wake*, London: Faber & Faber.

Jung, Carl G. (1966) 'Instinct and the Unconscious', *Collected Works*, Vol. 15, Princeton: Princeton University Press.

—— (ed.) (1990) *Man and his Symbols*, London and New York: Arkana.

—— (1992) *The Gnostic Jung*, ed. R.A. Segal, London: Routledge.

Kafka, Franz (1970) *The Trial*, Harmondsworth: Penguin.

Kearney, Richard (1988) *The Wake of Imagination*, London: Hutchinson.

—— (1991) *Poetics of Imagining: From Husserl to Lyotard*, London: Harper Collins.

Kermode, Frank (1967) *The Sense of an Ending: Studies in the Theory of Fiction*, London and New York: Oxford University Press.

—— (1973) *Lawrence*, London: Fontana.

—— (1990) *Modern Essays*, London: Fontana.

Kirk, G.S. (1970) *Myth: Its Meaning and Function in Ancient and Other Cultures*, Cambridge: Cambridge University Press.

—— and Raven, J.E. (eds) (1960) *The Presocratic Philosophers*, Cambridge: Cambridge University Press.

Larkin, Philip (1983) *Required Writing: Miscellaneous Pieces 1955–1982*, London: Faber & Faber.

—— (1988) *Collected Poems*, London: Faber/Marvell Press.

Lauter, Estella and Rupprecht, Carol Schreier (1985) *Feminist Archetypal Theory: Interdisciplinary Revisions of Jungian Thought*, Knoxville: University of Tennessee Press.

Lawrence, D.H. (1974) *Apocalypse*, Harmondsworth: Penguin.

Lévi-Strauss, Claude (1968) *Structural Anthropology*, Harmondsworth: Penguin.

—— (1978) *Myth and Meaning*, London: Routledge.

Lyotard, Jean-François (1984) *The Postmodern Condition: A Report on Knowledge*, Manchester: Manchester University Press.

—— (1992) *The Postmodern Explained to Children*, London: Turnaround Press.

McConnell, Frank (1979) *Storytelling and Mythmaking: Images from Film and Literature*, New York and London: Oxford University Press.

MacIntyre, Alisdair (1971) *Marxism and Christianity*, Harmondsworth: Penguin.

McLuhan, Marshall (1967) *The Medium is the Message*, Harmondsworth: Penguin.

Mali, Joseph (1992) *The Rehabilitation of Myth: Vico's 'New Science'*, Cambridge and New York: Cambridge University Press.

Manganaro, Marc (ed.) (1990) *Modernist Anthropology: From Fieldwork to Text*, Princeton: Princeton University Press.

—— (1992) *Myth, Rhetoric and the Voice of Authority: A Critique of Frazer, Eliot, Frye and Campbell*, New Haven: Yale University Press.

—— (1995) 'Making the World Possible for Art: Eliot, Modernity and the "Mythic"', paper delivered at 'Modernism and Mythopoeia Conference', University of Warwick.

Manuel, Frank E. (1965) *Shapes of Philosophical History*, London: Allen & Unwin.

Millett, Kate (1969) *Sexual Politics*, London: Virago.

Moi, Toril (1985) *Sexual/Textual Politics*, London: Methuen.

Morris, Brian (1987) *Anthropological Studies of Religion: An Introductory Text*, Cambridge: Cambridge University Press.

Morrison, Jim (1985) *The Lords and The New Creatures*, London: Omnibus.

—— (1991) *The American Night: The Writings of Jim Morrison*, Harmondsworth: Penguin.

Munz, Peter (1973) *When the Golden Bough Breaks: Structuralism or Typology?*, London: Routledge & Kegan Paul.

Nietzsche, Friedrich (1977) *A Nietzsche Reader*, ed. E.J. Hollingdale, Harmondsworth: Penguin.

Rée, Jonathan (ed.) (1992) *Talking Liberties*, London: Channel Four Publications.

Reeves, Marjorie (1976) *Joachim of Fiore and the Prophetic Future*, London: SPCK.

Rickword, Edgell (1937) 'The Cultural Meaning of May Day', *Left Review* 3: 130–1.

—— (1974) *Essays and Opinions 1921–1931*, ed. A. Young, Cheadle: Carcanet Press.

—— (1976) *Behind the Eyes: Selected Poems and Translations*, Manchester: Carcanet Press.

Ricoeur, Paul (1965) *History and Truth*, Evanston: Northwestern University Press.

—— (1967) *The Symbolism of Evil*, Boston: Beacon Press.

—— (1970) *Freud and Philosophy: An Essay in Interpretation*, New Haven: Yale University Press.

—— (1974) *The Conflict of Interpretations*, ed. D. Idhe, Evanston: Northwestern University Press.

—— (1986) *Lectures on Ideology and Utopia*, ed. G.H. Taylor, New York: Columbia University Press.

—— (1987) 'Myth and History', in *Encyclopaedia of Religion*, ed. M. Eliade, New York and London: Macmillan.

—— (1991) *A Ricoeur Reader: Reflection and Imagination*, ed. M.J. Valdes, New York and London: Harvester/Wheatsheaf.

Rieff, Philip (1951) 'The Meaning of History and Religion in Freud's Thought', *Journal of Religion* 31: 114–31.

Righter, William (1975) *Myth and Literature*, London: Routledge & Kegan Paul.

Rose, Jacqueline (1986) 'Hamlet – the *Mona Lisa* of Literature', *Critical Quarterly* 28: 35–49.

Russell, D.A. and Winterbottom, M. (eds) (1972) *Ancient Literary Criticism: The Principal Texts in New Translations*, Oxford: Clarendon Press.

Ruthven, K.K. (1976) *Myth*, London: Methuen.

Scholes, Robert (1974) *Structuralism in Literature: An Introduction*, New Haven: Yale University Press.

Segal, Robert A. (1987) *Joseph Campbell: An Introduction*, New York and London: Garland.

—— (1992) *Explaining and Interpreting Religion: Essays on the Issue*, New York: Peter Lang.

Simons, Herbert W. and Melia, Trevor (eds) (1989) *The Legacy of Kenneth Burke*, Madison: University of Wisconsin Press.

Spenser, Edmund (1966) *Poetical Works*, ed. J.C. Smith and E. de Selincourt, London: Oxford University Press.

Steiner, George (1969) *Language and Silence*, Harmondsworth: Penguin.

Stevens, Wallace (1984) *The Necessary Angel: Essays on Reality and Imagination*, London: Faber & Faber.

—— (1986) *Selected Poems*, London: Faber & Faber.

Turner, Graeme (1988) *Film as Social Practice*, London: Routledge.

Turner, Victor (1974) *The Ritual Process*, Harmondsworth: Penguin.

Vattimo, Gianni (1992) *The Transparent Society*, Cambridge: Polity Press.

Vernant, Jean-Pierre (1982) *Myth and Society in Ancient Greece*, London: Methuen.

Vickery, John B. (1977) *The Literary Impact of 'The Golden Bough'*, Princeton: Princeton University Press.

Warner, Marina (1994) *Managing Monsters: Six Myths of our Time*, London: Vintage.

—— (1996) *The Inner Eye: Art Beyond the Visible*, London: National Touring Exhibitions.

Watts, Alan W. (1954) *Myth and Ritual in Christianity*, London: Thames & Hudson.

Weston, Jessie L. (1920) *From Ritual to Romance*, Cambridge: Cambridge University Press.

White, Stephen Ross (1994) *Don Cupitt and the Future of Christian Doctrine*, London: SCM Press.

Winstanley, Gerrard (1973) *The Law of Freedom and Other Writings*, ed. C. Hill, Harmondsworth: Penguin.

Young, Robert (1990) *White Mythologies: Writing History and the West*, London and New York: Routledge.

INDEX